WOMEN IN POWER

The mission of the Council on Foreign Relations is to inform
U.S. engagement with the world. Founded in 1921, CFR is a nonpartisan,
independent national membership organization, think tank, educator, and
publisher, including of *Foreign Affairs*. It generates policy-relevant ideas
and analysis, convenes experts and policymakers, and promotes informed
public discussion—all to have impact on the most consequential issues
facing the United States and the world.

The Council on Foreign Relations takes no institutional positions on
policy issues and has no affiliation with the U.S. government. All views
expressed in its publications and on its website are the sole responsibility
of the author or authors.

WOMEN IN POWER

*Fighting for Democracy in an
Age of Authoritarianism*

LINDA ROBINSON

A Council on Foreign Relations Book

Columbia University Press
New York

Columbia University Press
Publishers Since 1893
New York   Chichester, West Sussex
cup.columbia.edu
Copyright © 2026 Linda Robinson
All rights reserved

Cataloging-in-Publication Data is available from the Library of Congress.

ISBN 9780231221740 (hardback)
ISBN 9780231563888 (epub)
ISBN 9780231565646 (PDF)

LCCN 2026010486

Printed in the United States of America

Cover design: Noah Arlow
Cover images: Shutterstock

GPSR Authorized Representative: Easy Access System Europe,
Mustamäe tee 50, 10621 Tallinn, Estonia,
gpsr.requests@easproject.com

In memory of my parents, Kathryn and Bill,
with gratitude for their inspiring examples

Success without democracy is improbable, and democracy without women is impossible. If we fail to act on behalf of the current and future female leaders in our world, the cost to our democracies will be too high.

—Madeleine Albright (1937–2022), former U.S. secretary of state

CONTENTS

CONTENTS

WOMEN IN POWER

INTRODUCTION

IN 1990, Violeta Chamorro became the first woman elected to lead a Latin American country. As a foreign correspondent covering the region's historic transitions from dictatorship to democracy, I traveled throughout Nicaragua, a country of cattle ranches and coffee fields, to observe Doña Violeta, as President Chamorro was popularly known, as she skillfully managed her war-torn country's delicate passage to peace. She disarmed the U.S.-backed Contras rebel force, tamed hyperinflation, and refereed disputes among her fractious coalition of fourteen parties. She set her chronically riven country onto a path of stability and stepped down in 1997 as the constitution required. Unfortunately, Nicaragua's democratic transition was aborted a decade later when Daniel Ortega returned to power and began two decades of increasingly repressive rule.

The contest between democracy and authoritarianism continues around the world, and according to all the major democracy trackers authoritarianism has been winning for almost two decades. Each year, more countries have been autocratizing than democratizing. As of 2024, 54 percent of countries on earth were classified as either authoritarian or hybrid regimes, which hold elections but lack essential features of democracy.[1] Populists on the right and the left arrive by the ballot box and stay on by eroding freedoms and undermining democratic institutions and norms, as Ortega did. The dominant source of authoritarianism today is this sort of creeping autocratization, not coups or foreign invasions.

As previous flagbearers of democracy, including the United States, take autocratic turns, the battle between democracy and authoritarianism has come to define world politics. But amid the fervent attention paid to this battle, the women who feature in it—whether as agents of change or targets of reactionary forces—have received scant attention. Some women leaders are being driven out by misogynistic authoritarians; others are successfully confronting them, as Chamorro did in the 1990s. Understanding the combined forces arrayed against women leaders as well as how some leaders are combatting those forces can help chart a path forward for both women's equality and democracy. This book explores both.

It is no coincidence that the decline of democracy has coincided with stalling gains for women leaders in government. That's because campaigns against women and gender equality form an integral part of the authoritarian playbook. Deterring half the population from competing for power is a tactically sound approach to gaining and maintaining control. The public policy scholars Erica Chenoweth and Zoe Marks have argued that authoritarians employ sexism and misogyny as tools to keep women from threatening their power precisely because women have proven, based on the scholars' own research on global democracy movements, to be a potent force for equality, participation, justice, and other foundations of democracy.[2] As a result, authoritarians seek to restore and reinforce historical power imbalances that are ingrained in property, inheritance, marital tradition, and other concepts, as the political scientist Valerie Hudson and her colleagues with the decade-long WomensStats Project have documented.[3]

The picture is clear to many women leaders who have been in the crosshairs. As former Danish Prime Minister Helle Thorning-Schmidt described, "Nationalist populists all have as a set piece some form of narrowing in women's rights and women's opportunity. At the same time as democracy is shrinking, we are also seeing that women's issues are actually the target . . . and this is a very, very difficult and bad cocktail for women worldwide."[4]

How have authoritarians and right-wing populists been able to discourage women from the political arena and roll back hard-won rights in many places? They rely on a global community that seeks to marginalize women leaders and opposes gender equality. They advocate controlling, coercive, and punitive policies—and, increasingly, open violence. Once-obscure groups and social media influencers support violence against women or commit it outright; such entities and their narratives have been embraced by politicians and public figures. As a result, violence against women in politics has become normalized. In a growing movement, Christian nationalist organizations preach that women should unquestioningly submit to their husbands. They even endorse withdrawing women's right to vote. White supremacist, xenophobic, and nativist movements attack women immigrants and women of color and seek to control childbearing choices to increase white births and limit populations of color. Members of these groups have gained footholds in governments around the world.

Digital technology has also played a central role. Women politicians are disproportionately targeted with massive waves of sexist harassment and abuse that are amplified by the algorithms of social media platforms and search engines, which promote violent and salacious material to keep users engaged—the more engagement, the greater the revenue stream. Artificial intelligence, moreover, has led to an explosion of deepfake pornography, a now ubiquitous tool to defame and delegitimize women politicians around the world. Far from remedying these defects, the major tech companies have reduced or abandoned efforts to detect and remove deceptive and harmful material, arguing that such measures restrict free speech.

Former U.S. Secretary of State Madeleine Albright, a lifelong crusader against authoritarianism, was one of the first to sound the alarm about violence against women in politics and how it erodes democracy. In 2016, she launched a global initiative at the National Democratic Institute called #NotTheCost: Stopping Violence Against Women in Politics. The campaign began documenting the scope and severity of the problem to help governments and civil society groups address it. "Historically, violence against women in politics has been a largely hidden phenomenon," the launch document noted, "but it is a real and grave concern for all those dedicated to strengthening democracies around the globe." One of the first global surveys conducted revealed just how ubiquitous it is: Worldwide, four in five women members of parliament reported receiving sexist insults or abuse, and almost half said they had been threatened with rape, beatings, kidnapping, or death.[5]

Such violence has been normalized to a high degree by political leaders whose crude and violent statements have created a sense of permission for the rest of society. Egregious examples include Donald Trump's comment about grabbing women by their genitals, an off-camera remark that came to light during his presidential candidacy in 2016 and that he later brushed off; former Brazilian President Jair Bolsonaro's remark that a female legislator was too ugly to rape, made when he was a representative in Brazil's national congress; and former Filipino President Rodrigo Duterte's call for female rebels in the Philippines to be shot in their vaginas.[6] As boundaries have eroded, credible allegations of—or even convictions for—sexual abuse no longer seem to affect a politician's standing. U.S. voters again elected Trump in 2024 even though he had been found liable for sexual abuse and defamation (judgments that he has denied), and the U.S. Senate confirmed cabinet secretaries despite accusations against them of sexual abuse.[7]

A spate of resignations in 2023 by women leaders subjected to high levels of abuse sounded the alarm of a worsening toll. The former Dutch deputy prime minister Sigrid Kaag rose to lead her party after a diplomatic career in the Middle East and Africa, never expecting that she would be subjected to death threats and online attacks—clocked at one every fifteen minutes—in her native Netherlands. After Kaag's two daughters began fearing for her life and begged her to resign, she left office with a public warning that violence was severely damaging Dutch democracy.[8] Scotland's former first minister Nicola Sturgeon and Finland's former prime minister Sanna Marin also resigned, denouncing the level of sexist attacks to which they were subjected. And New Zealand's former prime minister Jacinda Ardern announced that she did not have "enough left in the tank" to continue in politics after death threats against her tripled over the previous two years. Protesters hung nooses in front of Ardern's office. In her final two years, she received 90 percent more hateful tweets than any other politician in New Zealand. Helen Clark, who served two terms as prime minister of New Zealand from 1999 to 2008, said, "Jacinda has faced a level of hatred and vitriol which in my experience is unprecedented in our country."

There is no doubt that politicians make mistakes that can result in their losing support or elections. The problem is that women politicians are frequently and disproportionately subjected to sexist and violent attacks and often judged by a double standard. A study of Italian mayors based on twelve years' worth of data found that when women made the same decisions as men holding those offices, they were three times more likely to be attacked—and, as a result, significantly less likely to run for reelection.[9] The political scientist Farida Jalalzai found the same double standard at work in Brazil, where the first woman president, Dilma Rousseff, was impeached after being charged with corruption for a budget financing practice routinely used by her male predecessors.

A violent minority can thus eliminate women from politics. One in six women leave their positions in parliament before their terms expire; many of them cite sexist and violent attacks as their reason.[10] A third of women politicians in Sweden said that sexist hostility and intimidation made them consider giving up their posts, almost half of Bolivian women leaving office cited harassment and violence as a factor, and a majority of women in Australia said that they were less likely to run for office after witnessing misogynistic attacks against that country's first woman prime minister, Julia Gillard.[11]

The consequences are clear: Women's political leadership is facing unprecedented headwinds. Across the world, the rate at which women gained representation in parliament peaked in 2015 and then, with little fanfare, began to stall. The wave of leaders' resignations in 2023 was followed in 2024 by women globally losing more seats than they won, including in the U.S. Congress, to which fewer women were elected than at any time since 2010.[12] Women also registered a net loss in cabinet positions globally in 2024.[13] At the end of 2025, women comprised only 9 percent of the world's elected heads of state or government, 27 percent of the world's legislators, and 23 percent of cabinet ministers.[14]

Given that power is concentrated at the top, it is important to focus on the dynamics that have kept women out of top positions: 109 of the 193 United Nations member states have never had a woman president or prime minister. A major reason is that women who aspire to the heights of political power face stereotypes about how women cannot act decisively in crises and as commanders in chief, and that they lack the expertise to be stewards of a country's national security or foreign affairs. Because such claims speak to the core functions of presidents and prime ministers, they must be scrutinized to see where and how such allegations gain traction. In his 2024 presidential campaign, Donald Trump leaned heavily into this theme of presidential power as a male domain. He called Vice President Kamala Harris a "weak and foolish woman." He said, "She can't handle the presidency, and she certainly can't handle [Vladimir] Putin or President Xi of China. She will get overwhelmed, melt down, and millions of people will die, perhaps. This is not a charity event. This is an election for the biggest and toughest job anywhere in the world."[15] He added that world leaders would treat her as a "play toy" and "walk all over her."[16] He did not consult the record—which this book explores in depth—showing that women leaders are standing up to Xi and Putin and their ilk on a daily basis.

■ ■ ■

Why does it matter that women's gains in rising to positions of political power are stalling? If the main priority is to stop the rise of authoritarianism, why not leave dealing with its misogynistic aspects to a later date? Women need to be an integral part of the response to authoritarianism for several reasons. First, the more representative a democracy, the stronger it is—a point on which there has been wide consensus for half a century. Stopping the current wave of misogyny-infused authoritarianism requires dealing directly with how it undermines gender equality because such equality is a key aspect of the liberal democratic system that is under attack. Women can and should be part of the fight against authoritarianism alongside men because their nonparticipation is a sign of an unhealthy democratic system.

Enabling women's fuller participation in government is not just a matter of principle but also one of practical benefit. Women leaders can and do make significant contributions; incorporating their talents makes democracies more resilient. Wider competition produces a better level of talent. Although not all women leaders will be successful in governing, their records show that, on balance, they perform as well as men, including in what some perceive to be male-only domains of national security and foreign policy. Decades of research have found that women politicians also tend to support policies and investments that make countries healthier, more prosperous, and more peaceful.[17]

The argument for women leaders is not predicated on women being inherently better than men or bringing something unique to the table but, rather, that women have the right to compete in an atmosphere free of misogynistic violence. If it is assumed that governing talent is distributed randomly among the population, then women possess the same potential for governing well as do men, especially now that women have closed the gender gap in education. They bring additional perspectives and knowledge to the table, too. Owing to their socialization, women may have a greater understanding of family needs or of the costs of gender bias, which can be critical in crafting policies on education, health care, parental leave, domestic violence, and gender equality. But to win the highest offices, women cannot be single-issue candidates; they must persuade voters that they can address the entire gamut of foreign and domestic challenges, keep their countries safe, and make sound decisions in crises. They should not be judged by a separate standard but simply by whether they are good leaders.

In this contest between democracy and authoritarianism, and between those who believe woman can govern and those who do not, the outcome is not predetermined. A majority of people around the world say they believe in democracy—even if it leaves many disappointed—and that men and women are equally capable of governing countries. A fear that others will not support a woman, however, discourages much of the electorate from voting for a female candidate. In countries where women govern, the stereotypes have been eroded and women are seen as competent and capable. Some women leaders today have been extraordinarily successful in countering existential challenges and strengthening their democracies.

Having more women leaders helps chip away at sexism and misogyny in several ways. Their growing records of governance directly erode bias and increase public support for women leaders. Their examples also encourage other women to enter public life. For this role model effect to tip the scales further, their accomplishments should become more visible; many women leaders have been elected in smaller countries, which has kept their performances from being widely known beyond their regions.

Recent women leaders have shown how to counter sexism, deal with professional setbacks and failures, and approach the challenges of formulating and executing foreign and domestic policies. The cases of women who have faced authoritarian leaders, including those of China and Russia, are instructive, as are these leaders' domestic contests with populists who seek to undermine their countries' democratic systems. One of the most dramatic recent examples is that of Tsai Ing-wen, who was elected as Taiwan's first female president just as Chinese leader Xi Jinping was consolidating his power. Vowing to take over Taiwan, Xi launched continuous disinformation campaigns and advanced aerial, naval, and cyber activities to destabilize and unseat her. In response, Tsai, armed with years of experience in cross-strait relations, developed a comprehensive defense strategy, increased Taiwan's information resilience, and courted more international assistance. She also prioritized domestic reforms to strengthen Taiwan's democracy: mending a frayed social safety net, embracing indigenous groups, and passing Asia's first same-sex marriage law.

Women leaders in Europe have also faced down aggressors, including Russian President Vladimir Putin, by shoring up their countries' defenses and democratic resilience. Kaja Kallas, Estonia's first female prime minister, became a frontline leader responding to Russia's invasion of Ukraine and prodding Europe to bolster its defenses and wean itself off Russian energy. After two terms as prime minister, Kallas then became the European Union's foreign affairs and security policy chief. Maia Sandu, the first woman president of Moldova, has faced authoritarians at home and in Russia, which targeted her with a multimillion-dollar vote-buying and disinformation campaign that nearly derailed her. Against great odds, she fended off Russian subversion to become prime minister and then win two presidential elections. In the shadow of Ukraine's war and occupying Russian troops, she advanced democratic reforms in Moldova to stem corruption and prepare the country for EU membership.

Of course, women have also numbered among the ranks of authoritarians. The most notable recent example was Bangladesh's Sheikh Hasina, the daughter of the country's first president and the world's longest-serving elected female ruler. She presided over fifteen years of increasingly repressive rule until she was forced out by mass protests in 2024. Aung San Suu Kyi, the former leader of Myanmar, disappointed many when she took an authoritarian turn after spending decades as a democracy activist. Indira Gandhi imposed martial law later in her tenure as Indian prime minister. Women have also served in relatively powerless positions in autocratic regimes— a reminder that a seat in government can be a gateway to power and influence but does not automatically confer either.

Although not all women leaders are democrats, the records of the relatively small cohort of elected women leaders do not suggest that they are any more likely than men are to be authoritarians. Nor are elected women leaders any more warlike than men are; efforts to make that case fail to draw important distinctions between wars of aggression and wars of defense, the latter fought to repel an invader or aid an ally, as is the case with Ukraine today. Women leaders, whether they are of the left, right, or center, are neither all good nor all bad. They should, in any case, have equal opportunity to compete for power without having to face constant violent threats. The costs that misogyny imposes on them are depressing their numbers and should be addressed. In the fight against authoritarianism, leaving half the world's talent on the sidelines is a recipe for failure.

Chapter One

THE TANDEM CRISIS OF DEMOCRACY AND WOMEN'S LEADERSHIP

Women's rights are under siege. The poison of patriarchy is back—and it is back with a vengeance. Around the world, the masters of misogyny are gaining in strength, confidence, and influence. . . . The weakening of democratic institutions has gone hand in hand with backlash on gender equality. Anti-rights actors are actively undermining long-standing consensus on key women's rights issues. Where they cannot roll back legal and policy gains altogether, they seek to block or slow their implementation.

—António Guterres, UN secretary-general

AT THE OPENING SESSION of the UN's 2025 Commission on the Status of Women, Secretary-General António Guterres struck a somber note. On the thirtieth anniversary of the body's Beijing Declaration and Platform for Action on women's equality, the commission reported that a quarter of UN member states had moved backward, not forward, on gender equality in the previous year. Guterres pointed the finger directly at right-wing regimes seeking to roll back progress for women.

The current global surge of authoritarianism and far-right populism is explicitly hostile to women and women politicians.

Authoritarian leaders embrace sexist narratives that women belong in the home, not in the halls of power, because they are less capable than men and need the protection of men.[1] Authoritarians also mobilize voters who are antipathetic toward women, are hostile to gender equality, and decry efforts to address discrimination as unfair rigging of the system. Some of these leaders may not even believe in these narratives but use them to gain and maintain power; others do so to ensure that men remain at the helm of a patriarchal order.

This campaign against women and their roles in public life is becoming more powerful as authoritarianism and right-wing populism spread to more countries. By 2024, more than 70 percent of the world's population lived under authoritarian regimes, not only in closed autocracies such as China and Russia but in other major countries, too, such as Hungary, India, Türkiye, and Venezuela—where multiparty elections are held but where rulers undermine civil and political liberties, control the media, and manipulate government powers to maintain control. By V-Dem's rankings, there were ninety-one autocratic governments and eighty-eight democracies across the globe. Autocratizing trends have outpaced democratizing trends every year since 2005. In 2024, democracy declined in sixty countries and improved in only thirty-four.[2] As authoritarian leaders grow in number, so do their power and influence, enabling them to reach beyond their borders to tilt the playing field even in relatively stable liberal democracies.

Democracy has not always incorporated the concepts of gender equality and women's rights. But the "third wave" of democratization—which began in the 1970s after decolonization movements and, later, the dissolution of the Soviet Union—entailed growing recognition of women's rights and support for increasing women's participation in politics.[3] Scholars have debated the cause and effect. Some argue that women activists spurred the inclusion of women in politics while others believe that democracy provided a conducive environment for the expansion of their rights. Many think both forces have been mutually reinforcing. Debates over causality aside, most scholars agree that the strongest democracies are those that have fully embraced gender equality.[4] Historically, women's status has strongly correlated with basic components of liberal democracy, including free elections, the right to free association and assembly, and checks on executive power.[5]

What is not in doubt is that the trendlines for both women and democracy pointed upward for several decades but have now reversed. The following sections document notable cases of women in politics around the world in order to illustrate how and why women's representation is falling in backsliding democracies. They also identify the actions and rhetoric that authoritarian regimes use to oppose gender equality and depress women's representation and rights.

The notion that women should be part of governing structures was propelled by women activists. The first UN World Conference on Women, held in 1975, concluded that "a revolutionary change in the structure of society was needed to bring about the social and political liberation of women and to ensure their equal economic, legal and civic rights."[6] In 1979, the UN General Assembly adopted the Convention on the Elimination of All Forms of Discrimination Against Women

(CEDAW), which was subsequently ratified by 189 states. Governments began to take steps to fulfill CEDAW commitments and, although progress was uneven, the principle of women's equality became widely accepted.

In response to these advances, a global countermovement arose, led by both state and nonstate actors from conservative and religious sectors. The countermovement in the United States was especially strong, as Susan Faludi chronicled in her Pulitzer Prize–winning 1991 book *Backlash: The Undeclared War Against American Women*. The social conservatives who propelled the movement included several high-profile women, such as Phyllis Schlafly and Anita Bryant, who led the fight against the Equal Rights Amendment. The Senate passed the ERA in 1972, with President Richard Nixon's support, but it has never been formally adopted. Similarly, President Jimmy Carter signed CEDAW, but Congress failed to ratify the convention. While many democracies have enshrined equal rights for women in their constitutions, no such guarantee exists in the United States—making it easier, for instance, for the Supreme Court to overturn its own decision legalizing abortion.

Despite a surge of social conservatism in the United States and elsewhere, progress for women continued in the 1990s. The UN's Beijing World Conference on Women in 1995 put forward a Platform for Action that became a widely embraced road map for women's progress. By the end of the decade, 127 countries had created national agencies or ministries to address barriers to gender equality. The EU required new members to take steps toward gender equality, and international organizations made the establishment of ministries to promote gender equality a condition for membership. Committing to these goals and establishing laws and mechanisms to advance gender equality came to be seen as an essential feature of a democratic state. More than half of all countries adopted quotas to increase women's representation in their legislatures. Even autocratic regimes adopted such quotas and appointed women to consultative bodies, in order to burnish the image of their undemocratic rule.

As authoritarianism has risen around the world, progress in women's representation has stalled. The rate at which women won seats in parliamentary bodies peaked in 2015 and then progressively slowed, before taking a negative turn beginning in 2023.[7] The reversal became clear in 2024, when fewer women were elected to legislatures and fewer women were cabinet ministers.[8] The number of countries led by women fell by 20 percent between 2023 and 2025. This combination of indicators clearly signals that a half-century of gains for women political leaders is in jeopardy, and most of all at the rarefied top echelon. Moreover, this gap for women in politics far exceeds that in other spheres of life: According to the World Economic Forum, as of 2024 the gender gap in politics had been closed by only 22.9 percent, a fraction of the closures in economic empowerment, health, and education of 60 percent to 95 percent.[9]

Along with the evidence in the words and actions of authoritarian leaders, academic studies have found right-wing authoritarian views to be strongly associated with sexism.[10] Sexist attitudes are often a combination of "benevolent sexism," which sees women as needing protection within in a patriarchal system, and "hostile sexism," or misogyny, which is antipathetic toward women and attempts to prevent them from obtaining power or status.[11] A study of the 2016 U.S. presidential election found that "sexism powerfully predicted vote choice even after controlling for authoritarianism, partisanship, and other predispositions."[12] Right-wing authoritarians also frequently embrace religious, nativist, or other views that lead to restrictive policies toward women.[13] In another concerning development, younger men are less in favor of gender equality than past generations were. In a global survey in 2024, 60 percent of Gen Z men said that women's equality discriminates against them; only 43 percent of baby boomers said the same. This view may have helped spur a majority of white Gen Z men to vote for Trump in 2024 and may be tied to the antifeminism prevalent in the social media "manosphere."[14]

Anti-woman or authoritarian views are not synonymous with conservatism. There are conservative champions of gender equality and women's rights. Having profound concerns about contentious issues such as transgender rights for minors and illegal immigration—and seeking policy solutions for those concerns—does not in itself constitute authoritarianism, which is distinguished by denying basic rights such as due process, imposing unilateral measures without democratic processes, and embracing violent solutions. The war on "gender ideology" has become a vehicle for bigotry and demonization that has not been conducive to reasoned debate or to policymaking that is informed by medical professionals, science, and respect for individual human rights.

DEMOCRATIC BACKSLIDING AND THE DECLINE OF WOMEN'S REPRESENTATION

The combination of rising authoritarianism, declining democracy, and the women's arrested gains constitutes a global trend, albeit one with regional variations. The notable rise of far-right populism in Europe and the Americas has been closely associated with gender backlash and the stalling of women's representation, but similar examples exist in other regions. The climate for women in politics has grown generally more hostile as more authoritarian and populist governments oppose and overturn reproductive and LGBTQ rights, including by dispensing with laws curbing domestic violence or permitting same-sex marriage. They have dismantled ministries, programs, and funding for gender equality and for the adherence to international agreements meant to promote women's rights and prevent violence against women. This backlash to decades of progress is pursued by an increasingly organized community of political, social, and religious groups that work across national boundaries to advance their goals.[15]

CENTRAL AND EASTERN EUROPE: THE EPICENTER OF RIGHT-WING POPULISM

The most prominent cases of democratic backsliding in Europe occurred in Central and Eastern Europe, regions that also featured some of the most regressive policies on women's rights and gender equality. Hungary tops the list. The country's prime minister, Viktor Orbán, has governed since 2010, making him the longest-serving leader in Europe as of 2025. He has fostered close ties with Putin and Trump, who praised him as "a very great leader, very strong man."[16] Orbán's advisers even helped craft Project 2025, the blueprint for Trump's second term that contains many elements of Orbán's formula for expanding executive powers, targeting nongovernmental organizations, and undermining gender equality.[17]

Orbán's democratic backsliding coincided with his campaign against gender equality. Through multiple constitutional revisions, he consolidated power to govern for four terms. He reduced judicial independence, rewrote electoral laws, gained influence over state and private media, and adopted a "foreign agent" law to hamper nongovernmental organizations. By 2019, V-Dem deemed the government an electoral autocracy.[18] Orbán's 2010 constitution declared the traditional family model as "the basis of the survival of the nation" and marriage as "the union of a man and woman." The government has instituted a selective campaign to promote large families provided that they are created by heterosexual, married, middle-class couples. It has also outlawed changing one's gender identity, banned gender studies as an accredited field, and restricted the publication or broadcast of LGBTQ material that might be viewed by children.[19] A constitutional amendment passed in 2025 barred public LGBTQ events and declared that only two genders exist. Other decrees require the government to protect "Christian culture" and "Christian education" for Hungarian children.

This hostile climate has produced one of Europe's lowest rates of women's political representation. As of 2025, women comprised just 15 percent of the country's members of parliament and held no cabinet positions. Women represented 26.8 percent of total political candidates in Hungary in 2018; by 2022, that figure had dropped dramatically to 17.6 percent. Politicians and pro-government media outlets routinely undermine and attack women politicians, who are disproportionately harassed and doxed, commonly portrayed as foreign agents or opponents of "traditional values," and demeaned as weak, stupid, or unqualified. Facebook, one of the most widely used social media platforms in Hungary, did not employ fact-checkers to detect disinformation in Hungary for five years after it had adopted policies to do so elsewhere. Hungary ranks next to last in the EU Gender Equality Index. Orbán's policies were staunchly supported by Katalin Novák, who served as the minister of family affairs and later as Hungary's first woman president from 2022 to 2024.

Orbán also took his campaign against gender equality to the international arena. In 2020, he withdrew Hungary from the Istanbul Convention, the first international treaty to stop violence against women, which had been introduced in 2011 and signed by a majority of European states, including Hungary.[20] Other backsliding democracies, such as Türkiye, Bulgaria, Croatia, Czechia, Poland, and Slovakia, also withdrew, alleging that the convention promoted "gender ideology."[21] The objective of the Istanbul Convention was to provide legally binding standards to protect women against all forms of violence. Instead, Hungary, Russia, Poland, and other governments in Eastern Europe, Latin America, and Africa have waged a worldwide campaign against same-sex marriage, divorce, birth control, and abortion and have promoted traditional heterosexual marriage and the "natural family" in organizations like the World Congress of Families, which was founded in the United States and is heavily supported by Russians.[22]

Poland's right-wing Law and Justice party, elected in 2015, pursued many of the same policies as Hungary, including a draconian abortion law. The party lost parliamentary elections in 2023, owing in part to massive protests spearheaded by women and to EU sanctions levied against the country for degrading judicial independence and the rule of law. But Poland's new parliament failed to muster the votes to liberalize the abortion ban, and the president, who belonged to the Law and Justice party, vetoed a bill to restore emergency contraception. In elections in 2025, Law and Justice retained the presidency and promised continued deadlock on social reforms and other policies. Although women occupy 31 percent of parliamentary seats in Poland, the country ranks twenty-first in Europe in the Gender Equality Index—well below the average—owing to stalling progress over the past fifteen years in women's political, economic, and social empowerment.

Slovakia is another backsliding democracy in the region. The deeply polarized country reelected populist Robert Fico as prime minister in 2023 for a fourth time. He had resigned as prime minister in 2018 amid nationwide protests spurred by the killing of a journalist who had been investigating his government's ties to organized crime. Those demonstrations powered the election of Slovakia's first woman president, Zuzana Čaputová, a crusading anti-corruption lawyer, in 2019. She championed creation of a national crime agency and a special prosecutor's office that investigated Fico and other members of his party. While out of office, Fico publicly attacked Čaputová, calling her an "American whore" at a public May Day celebration in 2022. "The more of a whore a person is, the more famous they become," he added, in reference to the international recognition she had garnered for her democracy-building efforts during her presidency.[23]

In 2023, Čaputová announced that she would not run for reelection, citing harassment, death threats, and concern for her family. When Fico returned to office, the backsliding began immediately. He reversed Čaputová's anti-corruption measures, disbanded the national crime agency, the media, and government cultural institutions. Copying initiatives in Russia, Hungary, and elsewhere, he introduced limits on freedom of information and assembly and passed a foreign agent law to restrict NGOs. He realigned Slovakia with Hungary and Russia and cut off aid to Ukraine. For her remaining months in office, Čaputová fought Fico's attempts to water down criminal penalties for corruption as well as his claim that protections for whistleblowers were unconstitutional; the European Parliament concurred. Large protests erupted against Fico, who was wounded in an assassination attempt in 2024. Čaputová spent the last year of her presidency battling the country's democratic backsliding and retained her rating by the public as the country's most trustworthy politician.

Fico's undermining of Slovakia's democracy included creating a hostile climate for women and LGBTQ people. He introduced a draft law to amend the constitution to recognize only two sexes, restrict adoption to married couples, limit the ability to make legal gender changes, and require that educational content conform to "constitutional values." Women remain underrepresented in politics in Slovakia, holding only 23 percent of parliamentary seats. Between 2016 and 2023, women's candidacy rates fell from a high of 32.9 percent to 25.3 percent, a sign that women have grown more reluctant to enter the fray. The country ranked twenty-fifth of twenty-seven member states in the EU Gender Equality Index's measure of political, economic, and social power as of 2024.

RIGHT-WING POPULISM GAINS GROUND IN WESTERN EUROPE

Far-right parties have surged in much of Western Europe, propelled by both anti-immigrant and anti–gender equality campaigns. In elections across Europe in 2024, the far right won the largest share of votes in Germany, Austria, France, the Netherlands, and Czechia and gained ground in Spain and Portugal.

Spain's right-wing Vox party captured enough voters to become the country's third-largest party. It did so through sexist appeals, antagonism toward women's gains, and a pledge to return to male hegemony; two-thirds of its voters are male.[24] The party specifically targets aggrieved males by denying that gender discrimination exists and by labeling feminists as "feminazis" who, because they allegedly threaten the family institution, are undeserving of public funding. Vox also seeks to overturn legislation against gender violence on the grounds that it discriminates against men's civil rights.

In France, the far-right National Rally won its largest share ever, with 31.4 percent of the vote. A swell among France's far-right parties, including by the newcomer Reconquête, was matched by a second consecutive election in which the number of women elected to parliament declined. As of 2025, women held 208 seats, down from an all-time high of 229 in 2018. The National Rally gained women voters, largely on the back of its anti-immigrant platform and its incorrect conflation of violence against women with immigration. Seeking to appeal to more women, the party's leader, Marine Le Pen, had previously dropped her opposition to France's constitutional amendment enshrining the right to abortion, though the party has opposed the EU's adoption of abortion rights. It has also resisted measures to increase women's leadership in government and laws against gender-based violence. The surge in right-wing parties has also coincided with an increase in attacks on LGBTQ people in France.

German politics have also shifted to the right, as the far-right Alternative for Germany (AfD) gained historic ground in elections in 2025 to become the country's second most popular party. Like the National Rally, the AfD also features a woman leader, Alice Weidel, a lesbian with a Sri Lankan–born partner and two adopted children. Despite her personal choices, she supports the party's promotion of "traditional" families comprising heterosexual parents and biological children raised in conventional gender roles. Weidel maintains that she is a feminist, although she expresses that ideology mainly by criticizing the mistreatment of women in some conservative Muslim societies. She supports the mass deportation of legal residents of foreign origin. Only 11 percent of AfD representatives are women. Coinciding with the party's rise, women's share of seats in the Bundestag declined to 32 percent in 2024, from a high of 37 percent in 2016. Their leadership roles and candidacy rates have also declined, and their cabinet positions have dropped precipitously, from nearly half of the cabinet to just a handful of roles in 2025—a sad commentary on the state of women's leadership in Germany following Angela Merkel's pathbreaking sixteen-year tenure as chancellor.

Italy's first woman prime minister, Giorgia Meloni, has governed with a far-right coalition led by the Brothers of Italy, the party she cofounded. At home, Meloni's moves to curb gender equality and press freedom sparked protests. Although she had pledged not to seek a reversal of the country's longstanding legal right to abortion, she implemented other measures to reduce abortion access, limit registry to birth parents, and prevent Italians from seeking surrogacy abroad. Since the Meloni government came to power, women's representation in parliament has declined by 4 percent. She has strongly supported Ukraine as well as sanctions on Russia, unlike other far-right leaders in Europe, and as prime minister she has tacked to the center-right by moderating some of her previous positions. But her hostility to the LGBTQ community and the press, her ethnonationalist views, and her proposal to enhance the power of minority governments raise doubts about her commitment to democratic norms.

In 2024 elections for the European Parliament, women gained fewer seats than in the previous election for the first time in the body's history, reflecting the repercussions of the right-wing surge throughout the continent. The European Union has set standards for its member states on gender equality and democratic rule of law. If far-right populists gain increasing sway in European governments, member states could begin to push back against such standards and challenge their enforcement through suspension of aid to member states, as the EU has done to both Hungary and Poland.[25]

LAGGING RIGHTS AND LEADERSHIP IN ASIA AND THE MIDDLE EAST

The Middle East and North Africa region remains dead last in women's political representation, and it is no coincidence that it is also the region with the least democracy. Türkiye has been rated "not free" by Freedom House since 2012, as Recep Tayyip Erdoğan has consolidated power by making constitutional changes, taking control of the media, and imprisoning protestors, journalists, and political opponents, including his chief rival. As part of his growing authoritarianism, Erdoğan moved Türkiye away from CEDAW, spearheading a wave of withdrawals, and mounted attacks on "gender ideology." The share of women legislators has stalled at 19.9 percent since 2023 and is only 2.1 percentage points higher than it was in 2015, in part because women candidates are placed far down on party lists.

Afghanistan is a stark example of how democratic regression has reduced women's representation. The country's twenty-year democratic experiment ended with the Taliban's takeover in 2021, after which Afghanistan once again became a closed autocracy. The regime imposed draconian measures on women and girls that several human rights groups decried as gender apartheid; more than a hundred edicts virtually erased women and girls from public life. During the country's nascent democracy, successive parliaments included more than sixty women, and hundreds more ran for office. The Taliban has since banned women and girls from politics, most public spaces, and education past the sixth grade.

The lone woman in the Arab world to reach a top political post, Najla Bouden, was appointed Tunisia's prime minister by President Kais Saied in 2021, but he dismissed her two years later as he continued to tighten his grip on the country. The lone democracy to emerge from the Arab Spring, Tunisia had achieved remarkable progress; it had a new constitution that enshrined gender equality, a "zebra" electoral system whereby party lists alternate men and women candidates, and government-provided campaign financing. Women won 31 percent of the seats in parliament in 2014, a major achievement. But Saied then suspended the constitution, jailed opponents, and changed the electoral system from multimember to single-member districts, which reduced the number of women legislators by almost half.

No Arab countries in the Middle East were rated as democracies as of 2025, although women have gained visibility in parliaments and appointed political positions. Several Gulf states have appointed or elected women to national consultative bodies. Fifty percent of the United Arab Emirates' national advisory council are women. Kuwait elected a woman to its national assembly in 2023 but suspended the body in 2024. Iraq, Egypt,

Djibouti, and Morocco achieved critical milestones by electing women to more than 30 percent of the positions in their parliaments, but these legislators' impact on governing policy remains limited.

After the Middle East, Asia has the next lowest levels of democracy and women's political leadership, both of which have declined in the past decade. One prominent recent case of democratic backsliding in Asia occurred in South Korea, when in 2024 President Yoon Suk Yeol declared martial law and was then impeached. In his campaign for election in 2022, Yoon heavily courted the anti-feminist vote during a time of gender backlash. Organized groups such as New Men's Solidarity were reportedly responsible for spurring an increase in online and physical attacks on women. A survey found that 79 percent of young men in South Korea felt "seriously discriminated against" because of their gender.[26] Yoon played upon these sentiments in his campaign. He vowed to disband the country's Ministry of Gender Equality and Family and claimed that structural gender discrimination did not exist in South Korea—which, in fact, has the widest gender pay gap among developed countries and ranks 105th out of the 145 countries in the World Economic Forum's Global Gender Gap Index. Once elected, Yoon followed through on his pledges, cutting funding for women's equality and removing the topic from school curricula. Freedom House reported that misogyny, domestic violence, and other forms of gender-based violence were widespread in South Korea.[27] In recent years, inspired by the #MeToo movement, numerous women have come forward to lodge sexual harassment claims against prominent figures. After Yoon declared martial law, young women played a significant role in the protests that called for his impeachment.

Indonesia's presidential election of Prabowo Subianto, a former military leader, in 2024 raised concerns about democratic backsliding and decreased support for women's rights and representation there. Fewer women were elected to Indonesia's parliament in 2024 than in previous elections; they now comprise 21.9 percent of the body. Prabowo had been accused of human rights abuses while in the military. Following his election, he appointed few women to senior positions and significantly cut funding for gender-related programs, including the Ministry of Women's Empowerment and Child Protection and the National Commission on Violence Against Women.

Politics in the region underlines the point that women leaders are not necessarily democrats. Over the past half-century, Asia's dynastic traditions have led to twelve women serving as a country's president or prime minister because of family ties. Many of them, however, served only briefly, with limited impact, or else undemocratically.[28] India's Indira Gandhi resorted to martial law during her final term. Aung San Suu Kyi abandoned her lifelong activism for democracy in her native Myanmar after she became head of the government; she incurred global criticism for excusing the military's ethnic cleansing of the Rohingya minority and presiding over crackdowns on journalists and critics. Corazon Aquino, the first woman president of the Philippines, helped transition that country from dictatorship to democracy but was ultimately sidelined by her male vice president and defense minister.

LATIN AMERICA'S POPULISTS EMBRACE ANTI-GENDER EQUALITY POLITICS

In Latin America, populist authoritarians have come to power with an agenda to roll back women's rights. Argentina's president, Javier Milei, a populist libertarian, dismantled the country's women's ministry in his first week in office, in December 2023, and slashed spending aimed at reducing gender-based violence. His party has introduced a bill to overturn Argentina's 2020 legalization of abortion, which he called "aggravated murder," and has also removed "gender ideology" from government programs and school curricula. Milei rushed to Mar-a-Lago to be among the first world leaders to congratulate Trump on his reelection. He has since formed close ties with others in Trump's orbit, including Orbán and Elon Musk.

Also joining this club is El Salvador's president, Nayib Bukele, who won reelection in a landslide in 2024—a violation of the constitutionally mandated one-term limit, something his handpicked Constitutional Court did not contest. Immediately after his inauguration, Bukele ordered "gender ideology" to be expunged from schools. He has blocked bills to decriminalize abortion and recognize gender rights, sent police to break up feminist marches, and ended women's health-care programs.

In Brazil, the region's largest country, the right-wing populist Jair Bolsonaro was defeated at the ballot box in 2022. Although he was subsequently barred from office until 2030 and convicted of inciting a coup to overturn his election defeat, Bolsonaro retains a large following. As president, he rolled back gender-equality programs, cut funds for combating gender-based violence, and banned the use of the word "gender" in classrooms. An admirer of Trump who replicated some the American president's tactics—including seeking to overturn his electoral defeat—Bolsonaro routinely made sexist and defamatory comments to women politicians and officials. His backers in the legislature continue to press his policy agenda, including establishing penalties for women who have an abortion that are more severe than those for people convicted of murder. Seeking to forestall Bolsonaro's trial, Trump imposed 50 percent tariffs on Brazilian goods in 2025, posting on Truth Social that it was a "Witch Hunt that should end IMMEDIATELY."

In Venezuela, the opposition leader María Corina Machado fought for years to defeat the strongman ruler Nicolás Maduro. In 2023, she overwhelmingly won a primary election with 93 percent of the vote, despite receiving 60 percent more online abuse than any other candidate and even suffering physical attacks. The Maduro-controlled Supreme Court then barred her candidacy, leading to a substitute candidate taking her place. In the general election the following year, Maduro claimed victory despite data—compiled by a massive, Machado-led operation to collect copies of precinct votes—proving that Machado's opposition coalition had won.

Women in Latin America have gained a larger share of national legislative seats and top jobs than in any other region except Europe. The women who have ascended to lead countries have largely done so through family ties, such as Honduras's first woman president, Xiomara Castro, who is the country's former first lady. But increasingly women have come to power through their own political careers, too. Owing to strong feminist movements in the region, women have gained representation in legislatures, a phenomenon further supported by gender quotas. Once there, however, they continue to confront high levels of sexism and violence.

Mexico elected its first woman president, Claudia Sheinbaum, in 2024, as a successor to the left-wing populist Andrés Manuel López Obrador. Although she has earned high approval ratings for her handling of turbulent U.S.-Mexican relations, it was unclear if she would seek to reverse the substantial backsliding that had occurred during her predecessor and mentor's presidency, which led the Economist Intelligence Unit to downgrade Mexico from a democracy to a hybrid regime. Mexico is a leader in women's representation, with gender parity at the state and legislative level, though it suffers from one of the highest levels of femicide in the world.

LIMITED DEMOCRACY AND FEW WOMEN POLITICAL LEADERS IN AFRICA

Africa has been plagued by more coups than any other region, and as of 2025 Freedom House ranked only six countries on the continent as "free." African countries have been overwhelmingly led by men, many of them military leaders or strongmen who came to office and stayed for life. Most of the twenty-four women leaders who have been elected or appointed as heads of state or government have not exercised significant power. Among the very few exceptions is Liberia's Ellen Johnson Sirleaf, who served as president from 2006 to 2018. Malawi's Joyce Banda served as president from 2012 to 2014 following her predecessor's death, and as vice president before that; she performed well but failed in her reelection bid.

Women's representation in legislatures has grown in the past decade—buoyed by gender quotas in top-performing countries such as Rwanda, South Africa, Senegal, and Kenya—to match the global average of 27 percent as of 2025. However, these gains have brought with them increased rates of physical and online attacks against women legislators; in a recent survey, 80 percent of women politicians in Africa reported experiencing psychological violence online and 67 percent reported being subject to sexist behavior.[29]

The most dramatic fall has been in Nigeria, Africa's most populous country, where the number of women legislators fell by 19 percentage points in elections in 2023, continuing a downward trend that began in 2011. Women held only 4 percent of the seats in 2025, one of the lowest shares in the world. In 2019, Obiageli Ezekwesili ran for president in Nigeria, with development and anti-corruption credentials from her work as a former vice president of the World Bank's Africa department and cofounder and director of Transparency International. She had gained fame as Nigeria's minister of minerals and then minister of education, and later became a cofounder of the movement to free the Chibok schoolgirls kidnapped by Boko Haram in 2014. Still, she dropped out of the presidential race because of her concerns about campaign funding in Nigeria's oil-rich patronage politics.[30] Ezekwesili continues her advocacy as the chair of the global network Women Political Leaders. Her story is reminiscent of many women in Africa who have achieved high levels of success in international organizations but have found the doors to domestic political power guarded by men.

Women's leadership and democracy in Africa will be tested by forthcoming elections in countries where long-ruling parties are under pressure to liberalize the political arena. In 2021, Tanzanian vice president Samia Suluhu Hassan became the country's first woman president after her predecessor, John Magufuli, died from COVID-19. Hassan's initial moves as president to reverse the democratic backsliding that had occurred under Magufuli were encouraging. She released jailed political opponents and journalists, for instance, and lifted her predecessor's ban on political rallies. She also established a task force to help women ascend to more leadership positions; to combat the high rates of abuse and threats, the legislature passed Africa's first electoral law revision banning violence against women in politics.

Tanzania's democratic turn was short-lived, however. To maintain the party's hold on power, Hassan's government violently cracked down on the opposition, arrested the main leaders, restricted the press and civil society organizations, and disqualified the main opposition party from participating in the October 2025 elections. Despite election observers' reports of irregularities, Hassan was declared the winner with 98 percent of the votes. As protests erupted, the internet was shut down and hundreds of mostly young Tanzanians were killed by police and armed civilians.

The election in 2024 of Netumbo Nandi-Ndaitwah as the first woman president of Namibia marked a rare victory for women leaders in Africa, especially because the position is the head of both state and government. A veteran of the socialist SWAPO party, which led the country's independence struggle and has ruled for thirty-five years, Nandi-Ndaitwah previously served as vice president and in multiple cabinet positions. After her election, other women assumed the posts of vice president, speaker of the parliament, and secretary-general of SWAPO. Half of her cabinet ministers are women, too. She embarked on an ambitious plan of land reform and increasing education and job opportunities for the 44 percent of youth who are unemployed.

LARGE COUNTRIES POWER THE GLOBAL AUTHORITARIAN AND ANTI–GENDER EQUALITY TRENDS

A major factor in the worldwide tilt toward authoritarianism is the influence of many large, powerful countries that have slid far down that path. Seventy percent of the world's population now lives under authoritarian governments, which together control half the world's wealth, giving them enormous ability to exert political, economic, or military pressure on other countries. Russia and China, for instance, are entrenched authoritarian regimes; India, too, has been sliding into authoritarianism for more than a decade. The United States under Trump has taken alarming steps in the same direction. All of these countries' leaders project hyper-masculine images and pursue policies inimical to women's equality.

In Russia, Vladimir Putin has extended his brutal rule, which began in 2000, through a variety of maneuvers to bring the government, economy, and press further under his control. These include the outright killing of his political opponents. In addition to his deepening authoritarianism, Putin has cultivated a macho image, even posing for photos bare-chested, and fostered a climate of paternalistic sexism and hostility to women and LGBTQ people. He has promoted laws that have rolled back women's rights, jailed feminist activists, decriminalized domestic violence, and banned LGBTQ "propaganda." The Russian State Duma proposed outlawing feminism as an extremist ideology, and terrorism statutes have been used to sentence feminist activists to prison.[31] Putin called on Russian women to birth at least eight children each as part of a pronatalist campaign for "ethnic survival."[32] The Russian government—with the help of the Russian Orthodox Church and misogynistic domestic social groups such as the Male State—has waged continuous disinformation campaigns against women leaders outside of Russia, using sexist and demeaning language and imagery.

In China, Xi Jinping has steadily consolidated his power since he rose to leadership in 2012. In 2015, members of a group called the Feminist Five were jailed for planning a protest against sexual harassment, and the past decade has seen a government-orchestrated anti-feminist wave. Under Xi, who was once known by the nickname Big Daddy Xi, women have been sidelined from the highest levels of government: In 2022, Xi further tightened his grip at the Twentieth Communist Party Congress with a reshuffling that left no woman on the ruling Politburo for the first time since 1997. Under Xi's watch, China has conducted a sterilization and birth control campaign for Uyghur women and other ethnic minorities while mounting an aggressive push for Han women to have more babies, as Leta Hong Fincher eloquently chronicles in her book *Leftover Women*.[33] The government quelled a short-lived #MeToo movement in China and continues to severely repress feminist activists; in 2025, courts sentenced two prominent women activists to prison for inciting "subversion." Chinese state media also incessantly targeted Taiwan's first woman president, Tsai Ing-wen, with gendered slurs.

As democracy has eroded in India, the world's most populous country with 1.46 billion people, women seeking office there have faced increased obstacles.[34] Prime Minister Narendra Modi's rule has been characterized by rising violence against women as well as discrimination against Muslims, attacks on civil society organizations and the press, and the jailing of political opponents.[35] Owing to widespread violence against women and lagging gender equality, India ranks 129th out of the 149 countries evaluated in the World Economic Forum's Gender Gap Index. Women's political representation remains low, despite a government pledge to introduce gender quotas in India's lower house of parliament once a new census is conducted. Currently, women hold only 14.7 percent of those seats. (A third of local village council seats, on the other hand, have been reserved for women since 1993.) In a presidential election in 2022, Modi's preferred nominee, Droupadi Murmu, became the second woman—and the first person from a tribal community—to hold the largely ceremonial position.

The status of U.S. democracy became a central concern in 2025. The United States had been falling in democracy indices even before Donald Trump's 2016 election, but concerns over U.S. backsliding increased sharply with the violent riots and Trump's refusal to acknowledge his 2020 defeat.[36] The concerns became more pronounced following his reelection in 2024; his pursuit of expanded executive authority was buoyed by a Supreme Court ruling (*Trump v. United States*) that U.S. presidents enjoyed the presumption of immunity for their acts while in office. Fears of an authoritarian turn grew as he challenged congressional and judicial authorities, sought to overturn constitutional protections such as birthright citizenship and due process, directed government agencies to target opponents, and deployed National Guard forces to states over their governors' objections.

Trump's second term also made clear that sexism and misogyny were not incidental to his political playbook but animating features of it. When he declared that he would "protect women," he added, "I'm going to do it whether the women like it or not."[37] His campaign broke new records for demeaning women opponents; he called Kamala Harris "dumb," "emotional," and "crazy," and repeatedly mispronounced her name.[38] He said that she "put out"—a reference to giving sexual favors—and shared similar slurs and memes on his Truth Social account.[39]

Attendees at Trump rallies eagerly shouted sexist profanity, called Harris the "devil" and a "Jezebel," and wore T-shirts referring to her as a "hoe."[40] Trump literally broadcast a message of masculine dominance as he strode into the Republican National Convention to the James Brown song "It's a Man's Man's Man's World," followed by Hulk Hogan beating his chest and ripping off his shirt onstage. Trump's subsequent election showed how desensitized—or even welcoming—American culture had become to sexism in the public sphere.

From the first day of his second term, Trump began to roll back U.S. commitments to women's rights and gender equality. He disbanded the White House Gender Policy Council, which Joe Biden had established to coordinate gender equality policy across the government, and ended programs and foreign aid that promoted health care and also political and economic advancement for women and girls. He revoked the right of transgender people to serve in the military. The State Department disbanded its ambassador-level Office of Global Women's Issues and stopped reporting on violations of women's rights in its annual human rights report, except when it concerned countries conducting sterilization campaigns. The Trump administration withdrew from UN organizations that supported women's rights and refused to sign the annual declaration of the body's Commission on the Status of Women. The words "gender," "women," and "diversity" were purged from government documents, websites, and databases. Books on women disappeared from service academy libraries, and portraits of women were taken down from government museums and other official buildings.

Women's roles in national security were also gutted. Defense Secretary Pete Hegseth regularly broadcast his antipathy toward women. The two highest-ranking women in the U.S. military—Admiral Lisa Franchetti, the first woman to serve as the chief of naval operations, and Admiral Linda Fagan, the commandant of the Coast Guard—were dismissed despite long and distinguished careers. They were labeled "DEI hires," the same epithet used to discredit Harris. Hegseth had also inveighed against women serving in the military during his time as a Fox News host. "We need moms," he wrote in his book *The War on Warriors*, from 2024. "But not in the military, and especially in combat units." He dismissed two three-star women officers—his military aide and the chief military adviser to NATO—and transferred the first female vice admiral to lead the U.S. Naval Academy to a less visible post. By the middle of 2025, there were no women in the pipeline to become four-star officers, a chilling signal to send to a military in which women comprise 18 percent of active-duty members. As he announced in a vindictive social media post, Hegseth cut the Pentagon's Women, Peace, and Security program, mandated by a 2017 law signed by Trump, despite support for the program from senior uniformed leaders.

TRANSNATIONAL ATTACKS ON WOMEN LEADERS

Authoritarian populists' attacks on women in politics do not stop at the water's edge. Defamation and disinformation campaigns have increasingly become transnational. One such example is the violent opposition that transformed New Zealand's politics and caused Jacinda Ardern to step down as prime minister. The country was the first to grant women the right to vote, in 1893, and had elected two women prime ministers before Ardern, who became the world's youngest leader when she was elected at the age of thirty-seven.

Ardern, a progressive politician, came to power in 2017, shortly after the beginning of Trump's first term. She made empathy and kindness explicit themes of her government, leading many in the media to characterize her as Trump's antithesis. Her government was tested by a succession of crises, including a massacre committed by an Australian white supremacist named Brenton Tarrant. He killed fifty-one people in two mosques in the town of Christchurch and live streamed the atrocity on Facebook. Trump questioned why Ardern called him a terrorist. She replied by asking him to send a message of tolerance for Muslim communities around the world; Ardern was concerned that the viral video would spark other acts of violence. Trump replied that he did not think it was a very significant problem.

Trump's critiques of her continued during the coronavirus pandemic, even though New Zealand's health measures succeeded in achieving some of the lowest death and transmission rates in the world. In elections in October 2020, Ardern and the Labour Party won a landslide victory; Labour captured its largest vote share in fifty years, enabling Ardern to form the country's first majority government. New Zealand had vaccinated 90 percent of its population, but as the Delta variant took hold in 2022 many tired of the country's strict policies.

Approval ratings for Labour slid to 33 percent.[41] A decline in the polls was not surprising given the extraordinary circumstances of the pandemic era, but what was unprecedented was the flood of hateful and threatening rhetoric that engulfed Ardern. Violent demonstrations erupted and protesters chased her from public meetings. At a monthlong sit-in outside Parliament, protesters hung nooses outside her office; brandished Trump and American Confederate flags; displayed Trump, MAGA, and QAnon signs as well as Nazi swastikas; and issued calls to "drain the swamp."[42] Ardern declined to meet with protesters, saying, "When you see signs calling for the execution of politicians, that's not really a group that wants to engage in political dialogue." She added that the outcry "feels like an imported protest to me."[43] Other politicians and commentators agreed; they pointed to the Trump signs and other indications of outside interference, such as how a conspiracy news site hosted by Steve Bannon's GTV network was live streaming the protest.[44]

Trump piled on with his own disinformation, falsely comparing the surging Delta variant in the United States to New Zealand's sudden outbreak of nine cases after 102 days of having zero cases. "It's over for New Zealand," Trump kept repeating. Apparently resentful of the country's success, he said that New Zealand had been "held up to try and make us look not as good as we should look." Ardern defended her policies, and a medical journal estimated that if she had followed laxer policies, twenty thousand people in New Zealand would likely have died. The Maori population was especially vulnerable.

Many politicians in New Zealand denounced the malicious personal attacks. A member of parliament, James Shaw, directly blamed Trump for the chaos: "President Trump in the United States created a permissive environment for extreme-right . . . proto-fascist people, extreme misogynists, and so on, to operate in."[45] One study found that Ardern received up to ninety times more sexually explicit, toxic, or threatening abuse than other leading politicians did in the second half of 2022.[46] Researchers traced rape and murder threats made toward Ardern and her family to accounts "deeply connected to far-right, neo-Nazi, and accelerationist networks and actors—both domestic and foreign."[47]

Ardern's party, her husband, and even her young daughter did not want her to give up, but she decided that she did not have the energy to do a good job and announced her resignation in January 2023. In his first press conference, Ardern's successor, Chris Hipkins, called the treatment she endured "utterly abhorrent" and added that "men have a responsibility to call it out when we see it."[48] After her resignation, Ardern continued to devote herself to addressing extremist violence and counseling aspiring leaders interested in the new, kinder model of governing that she had promoted. In her memoir, she lamented "the hate, vilification, and extremism in the virtual world where we now spend so much of our lives" and the tendency of many politicians to amplify that hatred. She expanded the Christchurch Call, an international consortium she had founded to combat extremism after the 2019 massacre, to include a new focus on technology and misogynistic extremism. Ardern's experience brought attention to transnational defamation campaigns against women politicians and sparked research documenting exposing the perpetrators, global scope, and intensity of online and offline threats they are made to face. Violent language, violent threats, and violence itself were becoming ever more common tools to oppose policies—a dangerous sign of the decay of democratic norms.

Chapter Two

MAINSTREAMING THE FAR RIGHT AND VIOLENT MISOGYNY

WOMEN'S POLITICAL REPRESENTATION has been hurt not only by rising authoritarianism, but also by the migration of extremist ideas into mainstream political parties and political discourse. These extremist currents promote violent misogyny as well as coercive and punitive policies that disempower women. This normalization of misogyny has led to surging violence against women politicians and led many to shun or withdraw from political life.

Violent misogyny can appear on its own, as the unadorned hatred of women and the desire to harm or eliminate them. However, misogyny also appears in other forms. The spread of racism, xenophobia, anti-Semitism, Islamophobia, white supremacy, and Christian nationalism has been widely reported, but the role that misogyny plays in these various forms of bigotry often goes unrecognized.[1] In these extremist ideologies, women are portrayed as threats to a racial, ethnic, or religious community by asserting their right to make choices regarding marriage, procreation, and gender identity, and the response is to eliminate those women or force them to adopt the preferred choices.[2] While violent misogyny has been characterized as a gateway to far-right extremism, it is also an integral part of those extremist ideologies that seek to control women.[3] The embrace of these ideas within right-wing populism presents outright threats to women politicians and discourages many from the political sphere.

This chapter traces how extremism and violent misogyny have migrated into mainstream politics and normalized discourse around violence against women and proposals that remove or deny women's rights and political participation in the name of protecting them, the traditional family, and a given demographic group. These ideas have fostered violence against women in politics, creating untenable threats and a high psychological toll that have led many to shun the political sphere.

FEMINISM UNDER THE GUN

Norwegian terrorist Anders Behring Breivik is considered by many to be the father of modern-day right-wing violent extremism. In July 2011, he took a ferry to the forested island of Utøya, where, dressed in a fake police uniform, he methodically mowed down sixty-nine mostly young Norwegians attending a Labour Party youth camp. The motivation for Breivik's massacre is often described as anti-Muslim xenophobia, but this shorthand description misses the central role that misogyny played in his elaborate scheme to rescue white Christian culture. His primary target that day was Gro Harlem Brundtland, Norway's first woman prime minister, who served three terms and became a prominent international figure. Brundtland, who gave a speech to young campers that morning, was spared because Breivik missed the ferry and arrived later.

Breivik released a 1,500-word manifesto that blamed women for the decline of Western civilization and advocated killing women leaders to restore patriarchal dominance. Feminist women, he argued, were to blame for the immigrant surge in Europe: "The fence that has been taken down is Western patriarchy and masculinity, the ones who have taken it down are women—and it was originally put up to protect the very same women from 'external aggression by men.'"[4]

Brundtland's stature made her an ideal target. To Breivik and other white supremacists, she embodied the ills that women were perpetrating in Europe and the world. He called her "murderer of the country," a twisted play on Norwegians' frequent reference to her as "mother of the nation." Brundtland's global legacy included promoting women's leadership, launching Israeli-Palestinian negotiations that led to the Oslo Accords, and international development. A Harvard-educated doctor, she directed the UN World Health Organization and headed the Brundtland Commission that led to the UN Sustainable Development Goals for ending poverty, disease, and environmental degradation.

Breivik planned to handcuff her, read a list of her "crimes," and decapitate her on video. He wanted the ghastly spectacle to inspire the killing of women leaders around the world to compel women to leave politics and return to childbearing. Indeed, the Christchurch killer Tarrant called Breivik his "true inspiration" and repeated his preoccupation with procreation in the opening words of his own screed: "It's the birthrates. It's the birthrates. It's the birthrates." Right-wing political leaders also parroted the refrain, including a leading parliamentarian of Italy's Northern League, Francesco Speroni, who said, "Breivik's ideas are in defense of Western civilization."[5]

Even more influential was the tract "The Great Replacement," by French writer Renaud Camus, which argued that white populations were threatened by nonwhite immigrants with higher birth rates. In the United States, white supremacists used the term "white genocide" to claim that white people were being replaced through immigration, miscegenation, abortion, and violence against whites. The idea that women are perpetrating this depopulation of white people through their reproductive choices has gained increasing currency over the past decade, sharing the stage with anti-immigrant and other bigotry.

Over the past decade, the idea that women, and women leaders specifically, are to blame gained frightening traction throughout the world, becoming a standard trope in right-wing politics. Although "benevolent sexism" evinced in right-wing circles may seem a far reach from the violent misogyny of someone like Breivik, the shared rationales for action and violent rhetoric have blurred the lines as mainstream politicians and influencers embrace extremist views. Preservation of

"Western civilization" has become code for maintaining white Christian identity. Declaring an existential imperative for the continuation of their kind thus makes it necessary to control women's choices and behavior through the force of law or physical force. These ideas endorse violence, coercion, and punitive measures for women of color and other religions, as well as women who espouse gender equality and support multiethnic societies.

MISOGYNISTIC EXTREMISM MOVES FROM THE MARGINS TO THE MAINSTREAM

Replacement theory, with its implications for control and subordination of women, has gained growing support in the right-wing European and U.S. ecosystem, according to a study by the Institute for Strategic Dialogue, an organization that studies extremism.[6] In the United States, Tucker Carlson and other commentators propagated "replacement theory" on Fox News, and politicians began to use the term as well. Camus's tract spawned further publications that helped fuel the rise of far-right parties and identitarian movements in Europe. For example, Martin Sellner's Generation Identity became a continent-wide movement and shaped the platform of Austria's Freedom Party, a far-right party that received the most votes in 2024.

Christian nationalism is another extremist ideology preaching the subordination and subjugation of women that has found increasing purchase in the United States and elsewhere.

Its rise has fueled backlash against women in politics. Christian nationalists believe that women should be subordinate to men, who are the head of the household, and be devoted to the home. They believe further that the United States is a Christian nation that should be governed by religious doctrine and that Christians should exercise control over government and all aspects of society. These ideas are being propagated by a network of organizations and preachers who have founded hundreds of churches, schools, publishing houses, and podcasts with an international network stretching from Europe to Russia to Asia.[7]

One survey concluded that 10 percent of Americans are adherents of Christian nationalist views and another 20 percent are sympathetic to them.[8] U.S. Defense Secretary Hegseth belongs to one of these sects, called the Communion of Reformed Evangelical Churches, or CREC; he moved his family to Tennessee and enrolled his children in one of the five hundred schools it runs. The founder, Doug Wilson, and other CREC pastors endorse repealing women's right to vote and instituting a theocratic government elected by men who are the vote-casting heads of family.[9] Hegseth reposted a CNN interview with Wilson expressing these views with an approving message, causing an uproar.[10] He subsequently stated that he did not support repealing women's right to vote.

Hegseth was not the only prominent member of the Trump administration to voice support for the marginalization of women in government, including their right to vote. In a 2021 interview with Fox News host Tucker Carlson, then Senate candidate JD Vance specifically attacked women politicians without children as "a bunch of childless cat ladies. . . . It's just a basic fact—you look at Kamala Harris, Pete Buttigieg, AOC—the entire future of the Democrats is controlled by people without children," Vance continued. "And how does it make any sense that we've turned our country over to people who don't really have a direct stake in it?" In numerous public appearances, Vance promoted antidemocratic ideas, including an increased role for religion in government and regressive views about women's choices.[11] John McEntee, a Trump official who headed his White House presidential personnel office, made similar statements, posting on X just before the 2024 election that "we want only MALE voting. The 19th [Amendment] might have to go." His job at the White House and at Project 2025 included vetting presidential appointments and preparing a roster of "conservative warriors" for staffing the second Trump administration.

ENDORSING VIOLENCE AGAINST WOMEN

Violent misogyny is a central feature of the "manosphere," an online collection of anti-women groups that includes incel or "involuntary celibate" groups with names like Men's Rights Activists, Pickup Artists, and Red Pillers. The common thinking behind these groups is that attractive women (called Stacys in this community) control who gets sex and that men have been discriminated against and increasingly marginalized by feminism. According to some groups, men are therefore justified in taking violent action against women. Violent online discourse creates what one scholar has termed a "radicalizing milieu," which can inspire or incite physical violence.[12] Incels routinely advocate or threaten rape and other violence against women, and studies have found that men who engage in violence against women often frequent the manosphere.[13]

The first declared incel mass killer, Elliot Rodger, killed six and injured fourteen on the campus of UCLA-Berkeley in 2014 in a deliberately planned attack before shooting himself. Rodger's manifesto squarely identified his grievance: "all of my suffering on this world has been at the hands of humanity, particularly women." Rodger's attack inspired two other incel attacks in Canada in 2014 and 2020. Law enforcement agencies elsewhere have identified other incel attacks, but insufficient awareness of this motivation may have led to underreporting. The terrorism scholars Bruce Hoffman and Jacob Ware urged that "the incel movement should be of grave concern because of its increasing intermingling with violent far-right extremists and their own bedrock talking points of hatred and intolerance."[14]

Promoting violent misogyny has become a cottage industry for thousands of media personalities, podcasters, and influencers. One of the most prominent is the British American social media influencer Andrew Tate, with more than ten million followers on X, who openly advocates violence against women and asserts that they are "property."[15] Tate and his brother were arrested in Romania and charged with human trafficking, allegedly running a criminal ring to exploit women and rape. Far from distancing themselves from Tate, mainstream figures have embraced him and his toxic views. In 2023, the former Fox News host Tucker Carlson traveled to Romania to interview Tate under house arrest, saying his views about men "very much deserve a hearing." He has been embraced by other public figures and officials, including Trump's son Donald Jr., Trump's lawyer Alina Habba, and special envoy Richard Grenell, who reportedly petitioned Romania's foreign minister to release him from house arrest in Bucharest.[16] After Tate formed a UK political party called Bruv (slang for brother), Elon Musk endorsed him on his social media platform X.

Another violent misogynist who has worked to pull the Republican Party to the right is the white nationalist Nick Fuentes, who called himself "a proud incel" as leader of anti-feminist group called Groypers.[17] He advocated adopting Taliban-like policies, stating that "we need to go back to burning women alive more."[18] Fuentes's political activism included turning out followers for Stop the Steal protests and the January 6, 2021, riot and attracting Republican officials to his America First Political Action conferences. After he dined with Trump and Ye, formerly known as Kanye West, at Trump's Mar-a-Lago residence, Trump claimed not to know him. Both Fuentes and Tate, previously banned from Twitter, regained access after Musk bought the platform. On election night in 2024, Fuentes's post on X, "Your Body, My Choice," went viral with more than thirty-five million views, as part of a postelection surge in rape threats, sexist slurs, and calls for women to "get back to the kitchen," a blanket putdown of women that is often conveyed by kitchen-related emojis.

RISING VIOLENCE AGAINST WOMEN LEADERS

In this festering climate, violence against women in politics is rising around the world, even as the global homicide rate has declined.[19] The British government recognized political violence against women by including misogyny in its counter-extremism strategy and stating that it deserves resources equal to other terrorist threats.[20] Authorities blamed the social media influencers Tate and Fuentes for a widening embrace of violent misogyny among young men,[21] and the UK national police declared violence against women an epidemic following a 37 percent increase in violence against women and girls between 2018 and 2023.[22] Canada made a similar decision to declare violent misogyny as a form of terrorism by issuing its first prison sentence in 2023 for killings inspired by incel ideology.

The same year, the U.S. Secret Service identified misogyny and gender-based violence as potential indicators of mass killings in a study of mass attacks between 2016 and 2020 that found that nearly half of the attackers had a history of domestic violence, misogynistic behaviors, or both.[23] It concluded that "misogyny can play a central role in motivating an attacker to perpetrate mass violence, as well as engage in more prevalent acts of violence, including stalking and domestic abuse."

Women political leaders are targeted by violence at higher rates than women in general. A 2016 survey found that 85 percent of women parliamentarians and staff were subject to psychological violence, 44 percent were threatened with physical violence, and 25 percent had been physically attacked.[24] A subsequent survey of African legislators found that 42 percent of women parliamentarians received violent threats and 23 percent had been physically attacked.[25] Another survey of women legislators in Asia found that 60 percent received online attacks and 34 percent were threatened with death, rape, beating, or abduction.[26] The available evidence suggests that the worldwide rate of violence against women politicians is increasing, but the rate cannot be precisely calculated because globally comparable data is not collected.[27] The Armed Conflict Location & Event Data Project began to do so and found that violence against women politicians and activists doubled worldwide in one year.[28]

Despite efforts to criminalize violence against women in politics, murders of female politicians continue. The murder of Jo Cox, a British MP, in 2016, received wide attention for its brutality and connection to anti-Muslim and anti-immigrant sentiment. The attempted assassination of former Argentinian President Cristina Fernández de Kirchner in 2022 gained global attention as well. The killing of local officials Juana Quispe in Bolivia and Marielle Franco in Brazil helped spur legislation to criminalize violence against women in politics. Mexico also passed legislation, but nonetheless witnessed record violence against women in the 2020–2021 elections. In the summer of 2024, Mette Frederiksen, Denmark's two-term prime minister, was struck in the head by an assailant in the normally peaceful streets of Copenhagen, where senior officials routinely walk and bike to work.

Violent threats against women politicians have become an increasingly prominent feature of the American landscape in the past decade. Women in Congress are more targeted than men, and both Republican and Democratic women report death threats and stalking.[29] In 2020, a militia group called the Wolverine Watchmen plotted to kidnap Michigan's governor, Gretchen Whitmer, after Trump called on residents to "liberate" Michigan state from stay-at-home restrictions. Republican congresswoman Marjorie Taylor Greene was threatened with death, and Republican representative Nancy Mace was attacked by a man on Capitol Hill. Days after Kamala Harris entered the presidential race in 2024, a Virginia man posted online threats vowing to kill her and her family, pluck out her eyes with pliers, and burn her alive.[30] Three people had previously been convicted of threatening her with death, and one would-be assailant was killed by the FBI.

"WHERE'S NANCY?"

For years, Republicans vilified House Speaker Nancy Pelosi, the most senior woman in U.S. politics. Death threats against her mounted steadily and were vividly captured on television on January 6, 2021, when Trump-inspired protestors broke into and occupied her office on Capitol Hill. Rioters—some of them armed with guns, knives, axes, bats, and pipes—roamed the building, calling out "Where's Nancy?" Among women in Congress, she received the most violent threats, followed by Representatives Ilhan Omar and Alexandria Ocasio Cortez.[31]

In October 2022, a hammer-wielding intruder named David Pape broke into Pelosi's home in San Francisco in the middle of the night, calling out "Where's Nancy?" Not finding her, he bludgeoned her husband Paul, inflicting severe head and brain injuries. Pape was an avid consumer of conspiracy theories propagated by the QAnon movement that emerged in 2017, which painted both Hillary Clinton and Pelosi as leaders of a cabal of liberal elites bent on taking away people's freedoms and promoting pedophilia, cannibalism, and satanism. Pape planned to take Pelosi hostage, break her knees, and use her to lure and capture others on his hit list of elites. With his trademark lack of empathy, Trump made light of the attack and continued to call Pelosi "an evil, sick, crazy b—."[32]

DUTCH ETHNO-NATIONALISTS
TARGET WOMAN LEADER

The politics of misogyny and xenophobia also came to the Netherlands, where Geert Wilders, long the bête noire of Dutch politics, would win the 2023 elections with his brand of Islamophobic anti-immigration politics. The rising career of Sigrid Kaag, deputy prime minister of the Netherlands and leader of its second-largest party, was ended by far-right extremism. A diplomat who had been shortlisted as a future prospect for UN secretary-general, she decided to return to her native country to run for parliament. She was eager for her two children and her Palestinian husband to get to know the country of her birth and come to love it as she did. Instead, their experience made them fear for their lives.

Kaag's political skills were forged in diplomacy during a career of negotiating amid conflict zones. She served for two decades in high-profile assignments in the Middle East and in Africa, then returned to the Netherlands in 2017 to enter politics. She became minister for foreign trade and development cooperation in a rapidly ascending career. Kaag became head of the Netherlands' D66 party and led it to a historic second-place finish in the March 2021 elections. Widely seen as a contender for prime minister, Kaag was buoyed by strong debate performances, her pitch for a new leadership style, and concrete proposals to help the country emerge from the pandemic and address climate change in the sea-level country. She was tapped to become deputy prime minister and the first woman finance minister.

Kaag used her diplomatic skill to navigate the Netherlands' increasingly polarized and fractured landscape of twenty-one parties that spanned the ideological spectrum. She became a target of the far right, which had been gaining steam for a decade. Its leader, Geert Wilders, had made his name as the country's leading Islamophobe. His right-wing populist Party for Freedom called for enshrining Christian and Jewish cultural dominance in the constitution and banning Muslim immigrants to stop what he viewed as the Islamization of the Netherlands. Wilders described the D66 as "woke crazies, climate fools, Arabs, non-binaries" and called Kaag a "traitor" for wearing a headscarf on a diplomatic mission to Iran. Kaag staunchly defended her Palestinian husband and two children and spoke openly about the racism they experienced.

Kaag was astonished by the volume of increasingly violent round-the-clock attacks from the right-wing factions that were gaining ground in Dutch politics. They were not substantive critiques but vicious sexist social media campaigns with hashtags like #KutKaag (cunt Kaag), accusations that her Palestinian husband was a terrorist, and death threats against her. The racist and sexist insults trafficked in tropes about powerful women and about Muslim men and women who married them. After giving a speech, she would be inundated by messages calling her a "terrorist's sweetheart," "Palestinian hugger," and "whore" with disparaging remarks about her appearance, body, and dress. Kaag noted the contradiction between the Netherlands' liberal international image and what was happening to her at home. "We are a country that invests in women's and girls' rights all over the world," she said.[33] "But we apparently do not want to acknowledge that we still allow forms of misogynistic excesses in our own country."

One evening in January 2022, the Kaag family was at home when a young man came to their door shouting and waving a burning torch. She called the authorities, and the police assigned bodyguards to her and her family around the clock, mounted cameras outside their home, and began screening her mail. Legislators of the far-right Forum for Democracy party had been calling for tribunals and for politicians to be locked up, threats that Kaag had denounced as undermining the rule of law.[34] Kaag was shaken by the assailant's approach to her home and family, but she was prepared to carry on. Her daughters grew fearful for their mother's life, however, and in a TV interview they pleaded with their mother to resign. Kaag broke down in tears when the footage of her daughters' interview was played during a subsequent interview with her. She decided she could no longer subject her children and husband to the ongoing abuse and violent threats.

Kaag announced her resignation in July 2023. In November Wilders and his party won the most votes in the November elections, making him the kingmaker of Dutch politics after years in the political wilderness. His far-right views had gone mainstream and, with it, a normalization of violence. Kaag returned to the international diplomatic arena and became the UN senior humanitarian and reconstruction coordinator for Gaza. She regretted leaving her promising political career but said that as a progressive, a woman, and a wife in a mixed marriage she had a triple bull's-eye on her head. She told a reporter, "I did not expect to need the kind of security measures that I needed just to serve my country, a democratic and safe country."

Kaag's experience shows how rising extremism and authoritarianism have created a violent threat to women leaders. Sexist and racist threats were not the answer to disputes over immigration policy, and the xenophobic and misogynistic politics have damaged a country once known as a foremost liberal democracy. Kaag was found to be the most attacked Dutch politician, but she was not alone. The other three Dutch women who led political parties also received more attacks than other politicians, including death threats that doubled between 2020 and 2021—trends that were enabled and magnified by increasingly powerful digital technologies.

Chapter Three

TECHNOLOGY'S DISPROPORTIONATE TOLL ON WOMEN POLITICIANS

ATTACKS ON WOMEN POLITICIANS have been further supercharged by an unfettered social media industry and the explosion of artificial intelligence that has enabled new forms of harassment and harm, such as sexualized and violent "deepfakes" that have become a standard tool against women politicians. The varied uses of digital technology to threaten, defame, stalk, dox, and harm women politicians have exponentially worsened the wave of authoritarian misogyny that is driving women from political life.

ONLINE HARMS, REAL-WORLD CONSEQUENCES

The case of Sanna Marin vividly illustrates how the digital world can magnify sexism and have overwhelming effect on women's political careers. At age thirty-four, Marin became

Finland's prime minister in 2019. Less than four years later, fatigued with the sexism she confronted, she chose to leave politics. She and her women cabinet members were subjected to relentless, demeaning sexism that escalated after a video of her dancing at a private party was posted without her consent on social media. The video went viral around the world, eclipsing her many headline-making achievements at a critical juncture in Finland's history. She could not be seen simply as a leader, and a good one at that, but was instead discounted with the female adjective.

Marin's treatment was more remarkable given that Finland has a long record as a leader in gender equality. Tarja Halonen served as president from 2000 to 2012. But as occurred elsewhere, Finland's politics began to shift as the far-right Finns Party gained traction with its anti-immigrant, ethnonationalist, and socially conservative positions, mirroring the trend in much of Europe. Marin experienced this shift personally as she reached the heights of Finnish politics.

Marin became politically active as a teenager, joining the Social Democrats to promote more rapid government action on climate change. She won her first race in local government in 2012 and quickly gained attention through her forthright speeches, solution-oriented proposals, and crisp management style as chair of the Tampere city council. She then ran for parliament in 2015, introducing herself on the national stage as coming from a "rainbow family," raised by her mother and her female partner.

When Marin became prime minister in 2019, she began to experience regular attacks from online trolls. Like most millennials, Marin was comfortable with life online. As prime minister, she posted photos of her daily life with her partner and young child along with photos and clips of her carrying out official duties. She welcomed the opportunity to share the experience with her followers on Instagram. But she was unprepared for what became a vehicle of defamation and delegitimization of her as a political leader. Constant barrages from the Finns Party were joined by those across the Gulf of Finland from Estonia's far-right EKRE party, whose leader called her a "shopgirl" because she had worked in a clothing store while attending college.

Marin formed a coalition government of five parties that all happened to be led by women—a first for Finland. She was proud of the women who surrounded her, because they were ready to do the job, but it would become a fixation for many. Two months after taking office, the COVID-19 pandemic quickly tested them. The government performed well, rapidly issuing emergency measures, travel guidelines, and economic aid to cushion the blow, and successfully adapted the country's policies to remote and hybrid functions. But Marin and her colleagues could not get away from the relentless focus on their identity rather than their performance in the job and the issues confronting the country. One of the cabinet ministers, who was pregnant, was asked how she would fulfill her duties while pregnant and after childbirth—this in a country with national paid leave for both parents. Questions in press interviews invariably revolved around gender and age, not matters of state, as in a famous press conference Marin held with Ardern in New Zealand, where a reporter implied that they were meeting for personal reasons as women of similar age rather than in their governing capacities.

The ongoing avalanche of sexist and profane social media commentary was significant enough to prompt investigation from the NATO Center on Strategic Communications. It found that among Marin's cabinet of eleven women and eight men, the women received ten times more abuse than the men.[1] Derided as the "lipstick cabinet" and the "tampax team," the women, the study concluded "were overwhelmingly victimised by misogynistic abuse attacking their values, demeaning their decision-making skills, and questioning their leadership abilities."[2] A typical tweet directed at Marin said: "How do you manage to spew out such dreadful sh*t all the time, you left-wing hag? Go and bake something or load the washing machine. Empty-headed left- winger. You clearly have no clue how to manage this situation." The gendered criticism was ad hominem, rather than substantive, no matter what the topic.

Marin grew more troubled by the continued sexist and baseless attacks on her as the country confronted a national security crisis following Russia's attack on Ukraine in February 2022. Finland, as the country with the longest land border with Russia, was uniquely vulnerable in this moment. It had historically relied on a policy of neutrality to fend off Russian aggression, but the full-scale invasion of Ukraine raised the prospect that Finland could be next. Russia employed a variety of hybrid warfare tactics to destabilize Helsinki, including disinformation, cyber intrusions, and waves of migrants pushed across their shared border. Although Finland had a highly developed "total defense" strategy for mobilizing its society against Russian intervention, Marin and her government realized that additional measures were needed. They proposed that Finland petition to join NATO as the ultimate security umbrella against Putin's revanchist policies and relinquish its long-held policy of neutrality. That decision carried risks, as it might prompt further aggression from Russia, which was used to having the Finnish buffer between it and NATO countries. Marin was convinced that joining NATO was essential for the country's security, but the people had to be convinced.

As leader of the left, Marin was a key voice in persuading the progressive parties most wedded to neutrality to cast their vote to join NATO. The Finnish public rallied to her arguments and agreed to the sea change in its national security policy. In March 2022, 60 percent favored joining NATO, rising to 78 percent eight months later.[3] Marin also became a prominent international advocate for aid to Ukraine and a firm stand against Russia. At the World Economic Forum in Davos, she called for robust support for Ukraine and rejected calls for a negotiated settlement, saying that democracies needed to band together to resist authoritarianism. In an on-stage interview with Fareed Zakaria, she curtly rejected his suggestion of the need to make concessions, telling him that "all that is needed to end the war is for Russia to leave Ukraine."

Finland's NATO application was accepted, and the country navigated the accession process in record time. Despite that historic event and the prospect of greater security for Finland, the public spotlight on Marin's personal life continued to eclipse recognition of her performance as prime minister. The video of Marin dancing at a private party with friends, which went viral after an attendee posted it online, continued to be the most cited feature of her life long after August 2022. Political opponents excoriated her for behavior unbecoming the prime minister, and thousands of social media posts questioned her fitness for office. Some accused her of using drugs, which she denied. To dampen the spiraling furor, she took a drug test, which she passed. Marin stoutly defended her right to be a "human" and have fun.

Marin won her seat and more votes for her Social Democrats in April 2023, but the far-right Finns Party surged to an all-time high in a tight race among the three top parties. The Finns' popularity reflected the growing phenomenon of misogyny in Finnish politics. Marin ruled out joining a coalition government that included the Finns. She could have stayed in Parliament in the opposition but decided to resign because she was tired of the daily sexist barrage. "My endurance has been put to the test," Marin said. "These have been exceptionally difficult years and difficult times."[4]

In her final speech to her party, Marin walked onstage to the Aretha Franklin song "Respect," an implicit rebuke to the troll world. She focused her words on what she saw as the vital task at hand: support for Ukraine's defense and its reconstruction and standing up to Russia. "Russia and its representatives must be held accountable for the illegal crime of aggression, war crimes and the consequences of war," she said.[5] She remained unbowed, and even defiant, following her departure from politics. She encouraged her one million Instagram followers to embrace the model of millennial leadership she represented and cooperated with a filmmaker to produce a documentary for HBO Max about her government titled *The First Five.* In it, she and her four fellow party leaders recount both the sexism and their achievements as the first coalition government of five women-led parties. "I wanted to show the younger generation, especially young women, that you can be yourself," she said. "You don't have to become something else; you don't have to be an older man. We need diversity. We don't need more gray-suited people."[6]

Like Ardern, Marin continued to make her mark on international issues and provide lessons from her experience. She joined former British Prime Minister Tony Blair's Institute for Global Change to advise governments on democratic reform, climate action, and policy implementation. Former President Halonen lamented, in remarks to the Reykjavik Global Summit shortly after Marin departed office, that Marin had left government too soon. What had changed in the seven years between their respective tenures at Finland's helm? One of the key differences was a shift in the political environment that was supercharged by a permanent onslaught from the virtual world. It is still underappreciated how digital technology has the power to hijack a leader's message and very identity, in devastating ways for women in particular. A thought experiment: Would a video of a man dancing have ruined his career?

PUSHING WOMEN OUT OF OFFICE

Martin Chungong, the secretary-general of the Inter-Parliamentary Union, became one of the most visible champions of gender equality in politics after taking the helm at IPU in 2014. Alarmed by what he was hearing from women parliamentarians, he commissioned a series of global surveys that established that almost half of women parliamentarians are threatened with death, rape, beatings, or abduction, and a quarter are physically assaulted.[7] These are persistent trends that prevail across Europe, Africa, and Asia.[8]

These levels of violence are disproportionately experienced by women in politics, at roughly twice the rate of women in general. A 2021 survey by the Economist Intelligence Unit found that 82 percent of women in politics have personally experienced online violence compared to 38 percent of all women; these attacks range from sexism or sexual violence to harassment, stalking, hate speech, doxing, misinformation, defamation, video or image-based abuse, and violent threats.[9]

Women in politics also receive far more gendered online attacks than men. A 2021 Pew Research Center survey found that 47 percent of women reported online sexist abuse versus 18 percent of men. A study based on Twitter records found that Hillary Clinton received twice as many hateful tweets as Bernie Sanders in her 2016 presidential primary bid, and analysis of social media in national-level races in Australia, Canada, and the United Kingdom saw similar results.[10] In the 2020 campaign, Kamala Harris, as the Democratic vice presidential candidate, received four times as much online abuse as her male Republican opponent, Mike Pence. Other studies found much higher rates of disproportionality: As noted previously, women cabinet members in Finland were attacked at ten times the rate of their male counterparts.

Women of color who are politicians receive by far the most verbal abuse and specific threats of harm. In 2018, an Amnesty International global survey found that women from minority groups suffered 34 percent more online abuse than their white counterparts.[11] Studies of the 2020 and 2024 U.S. elections determined that women of color received four times more sexist abuse and threats than white women candidates and that Black women candidates were the most targeted of all.[12]

The abuse and threats are causing women to step back from office. A study by the Finnish government found that 28 percent of the women attacked said they would not seek office again. In 2019, eighteen women announced they would not run for reelection to the British Parliament, citing the threats and abuse they had received; they included Conservative Party members and two cabinet ministers, Amber Rudd and Nicky Morgan. Tory women serve an average of ten years less than their male counterparts. Heidi Allen, who resigned over what she called "the nastiness and intimidation that has become commonplace," said, "Nobody in any job should have to put up with threats, aggressive emails, being shouted at in the street, sworn at on social media, nor have to install panic alarms at home."[13]

Prime Minister Theresa May sought to stem the growing level of online hate directed at women politicians and presented an internet safety strategy, to little effect.[14] Gender envoys from the United States, Australia, and elsewhere have reported that women they met around the world were reluctant to consider a career in politics because of the vitriolic nature of social media. These anecdotal soundings are backed up by a

Plan International survey that found that one in five younger women retreated from political engagement after online attacks.[15]

Detailed reports from the organization #ShePersisted provided myriad examples of tactics used to discredit and delegitimize women politicians in Hungary, Türkiye, Brazil, Italy, Tunisia, and Moldova, including misogynistic and sexualized language and images, threats of violence, and tactics to undermine and depict women as unfit for leadership.[16] In 2023, the UN rapporteur for human rights also documented a pattern of politically motivated attacks on women politicians that aimed to drive women "out of public spaces and places of power" with the "overall objective to undermine democracy."[17] The report called for official recognition of "gendered disinformation" as a deliberate method to reduce women's political leadership.

The attacks are not only online or offline but a mutually reinforcing continuum of violence. Digital technology, including spyware and tracking devices in appliances, enable stalking, surveillance, doxing, and other forms of intimidation that in turn facilitate physical stalking and physical attacks. And online attacks, even without a physical attack, cause lasting trauma, including depression, suicide, and withdrawal from the public arena.[18]

Online attacks create a devastating effect through volume, speed, and persistence. Online misogyny is often expressed more crudely and more openly on social networks because of anonymity or distance from the victims, with more graphic, vitriolic, and violent language than occurs in many face-to-face exchanges.[19] Online communities can also wage mob assaults that number in the tens of thousands, often exponentially increased through automated bots. One survey of 778 women politicians and journalists found they received an abusive tweet on average every thirty seconds.[20]

I heard firsthand accounts of the damaging and vitriolic attacks women politicians suffer during a March 2023 meeting of global women parliamentarians, organized by the Women Political Leaders nonprofit organization, at Microsoft's office in midtown Manhattan. The goal was to bring the experience of women politicians directly to senior Microsoft executives. As the discussion moved around the table, woman after woman provided personal testimony and read verbatim transcripts of social media posts that they received on a daily or hourly basis. European Parliament member Lucia Nicholsonova of Slovakia read a sample attack from a sender who threatened to rape, sodomize, and mutilate her in "every orifice" of her body before killing her, to ensure she would never play any role in Slovakia again. Nicholsonova, who had been a journalist before entering politics and rising to become deputy speaker of the Slovakian Parliament, had left Bratislava for what she deemed a less toxic political environment in Brussels, where the European Parliament is seated. But the onslaught of online abuse followed her.

AI SUPERCHARGES THE HARM

The advent of generative artificial intelligence, which fabricates text, images, and video, has produced an exponential increase in online attacks against women politicians. The AI forms of violence are especially devastating: lifelike images, video, and audio lend powerful effect to efforts to humiliate, defame, and discredit women. During the 2024 presidential election campaign, Kamala Harris was subjected to dozens of deepfakes. In one fake election ad, shared by Elon Musk and viewed more than 150 million times, a synthetic version of Harris's voice says, "I was selected because I'm the ultimate diversity hire," over real and manipulated images of her public appearances.[21] Another deepfake of Harris, posted the after her first campaign rally, portrayed her as a prostitute, one of a constant stream of lifelike but false images, videos, and audio of her that continued until election day.[22]

These graphic, sexualized, and often violent images are used against women far more often than men, damaging their credibility as candidates and leaders. They play into widely held stereotypes that women are unsuited to lead countries and inflict permanent damage to their reputations. The images live on in the ether forever, with little effective response from governments or tech companies.

Deepfake porn overwhelmingly targets women, which is not surprising since the porn industry, the largest single segment of the internet by far, also predominantly features women. Deepfake porn first appeared in 2017, but its growth has been rapid. A 2023 report by the cybersecurity firm Security Hero found that 95 percent of deepfake videos are nonconsensual pornography depicting women and that the volume had increased by 550 percent since 2019.[23] Downloadable software allows anyone to create images and videos and clone voices in seconds, and programs like DeepNude allows users to strip clothes from images of real people, making them appear naked. The material is exploding across the internet; the cybersecurity firm Graphika reported that propagation of deepfake porn on X and Reddit increased by more than 2,000 percent in 2023.[24]

The use of deepfake porn against women in politics, and particularly those holding or aspiring to senior positions, has become a ubiquitous tactic used everywhere from England to Liberia to Thailand. Proliferating deepfakes of women British parliamentarians across the political spectrum caused Parliament to rush a bill to the floor in 2024.[25] German Foreign Minister Annalena Baerbock was targeted with a crude deepfake image in 2021 as she launched her bid to become the German chancellor; the image, depicting her as a prostitute, was captioned "I was young, I needed the money."[26] An analysis of the attacks and Baerbock's falling poll numbers concluded that the attacks had had a dramatic effect. Baerbock faced an ongoing stream of fake videos, accusations of pedophilia, and a fake story of her and an "African gigolo."[27]

Women in the U.S. Congress have also been attacked by deepfake porn. Videos of twenty-five female representatives were readily available through more than 35,000 online listings, and even after requests for their removal, search engines still brought them up.[28] Women at all levels of government are targeted. A young Florida councilwoman, Sabrina Javellana, withdrew from politics despite a promising early career after deepfakes appeared following her election in 2018.[29] Even after Javellana decided not to run for reelection, the deepfakes continued to proliferate.

PROPAGATING HATE

Online attacks on women are caused in the first instance by those who perpetrate them, but the design of online platforms and services amplifies salacious and hateful material—even to those who do not search for it—through algorithms designed to maximize clicks and retain people's attention. Social media platforms, message boards and apps, and search engines are complicit in creating viral propagation systems through algorithms and recommender systems that serve up inflammatory material to keep people scrolling and build profits.

Artificial intelligence models have been trained on vast amounts of violent, sexist, racist, and false data that is ingested from the internet. The single biggest product on the internet is pornography, which accounts for one-third of all traffic and is devoted to the objectification and exploitation of women. AI chatbots quickly learn from and mimic what they have been fed, leading to automated propagation of misogyny. Producing curated data sets of verified information is expensive and time-consuming, so companies have eschewed efforts to do so. The result is that women are being affected far more than anyone else, with little chance that this will change.

Tools have been developed that directly harm women and people of color. For example, AI-driven systems such as facial recognition software have been found to be deeply biased because of bias in the training data, thereby replicating existing societal bias and errors.[30] Amazon's employee recruitment tool recommended men rather than women because it was trained on a historical dataset of predominantly male hires. Health-care decision-making systems based on AI made similar errors because of built-in biases that prejudice diagnosis and coverage of women's illnesses. The fact that models replicate implicit and unrecognized bias in the training data often goes undetected because the validation process relies on the same uncurated data. Without a different approach to developing AI, the industry will continue releasing products that cause serious real-life harm.

Although some tech companies have policies against hate speech, abuse, and harassment, other platforms such as 4chan and Telegram place few if any constraints on users. For companies with policies, response time to user reports of abuse is often slow. Even companies with codes of conduct rarely make them specific to slang, coded language, and memes of gendered abuse that often differ by country, complicating efforts to detect and address it. Content moderators are often contract employees, scarce in number, and not hired at all in small foreign countries.

Independent, third-party fact-checking has been abandoned by many of the largest companies in the name of free speech. Following Musk's abandonment of content moderation, Mark Zuckerberg announced that he would adopt X's model of Community Notes, which did little to flag or filter false or harmful information. In a January 2025 announcement, Zuckerberg acknowledged as much, saying that they would catch "less bad stuff" in the name of free speech. The company then published new rules that specifically permitted various types of hate speech about women and LGBTQ people and stated that it would use automated filtering systems to screen only for child sexual abuse material and terrorism.

The burden of safety thus falls primarily on the user, but the design of most platforms, applications, and search engines does not facilitate safety through transparent and easy-to-use features. Default settings often do not prioritize privacy and are opaque or difficult to manage. Companies require users to report individual attacks, which is impossible during a swarm attack of hundreds or thousands of posts or shares. Many services have become less transparent and less accountable. Independent evaluations of platforms and servers are difficult or impossible as platforms such as X restrict API access and do not provide gender-disaggregated data to enable researchers to evaluate how algorithms and machine learning models are performing in addressing gender abuse.

Piecemeal, episodic, and after-the-fact efforts to address online harm have proven highly inadequate. When Reddit closed a deepfake porn subreddit, for example, the group simply migrated to the platform Discord.[31] A particularly heinous example of the online and offline harm inflicted through encrypted platforms such as Discord and Telegram involved an anonymous online club called 764 with thousands of young men on three continents who lured young girls into sharing revealing information, blackmailed them, and then coerced them into cutting and wounding themselves while being filmed online.[32] Such groups have renamed themselves and changed platforms and used various other means to evade law enforcement efforts.

RESISTANCE TO REGULATION

Despite growing publicity of deepfake porn attacks, social media companies and software creators have resisted taking safety measures. For years, the biggest platforms have insisted they provide a service and are, therefore, not publishers, meaning they have no editorial responsibility for the content on their sites. Methods exist to reduce the risks, but many tech companies are reluctant to use watermarks or labels to indicate artificially generated content or to adopt industrywide rules to take down content and deplatform repeat abusers.

Even well-intentioned companies with clear guidelines for handling online content find it difficult to detect and take down harmful material before it goes viral. Today's whack-a-mole approach leaves companies chasing an exponentially expanding set of targets. A more proactive approach in which companies identify and shut down habitual mass propagators has had greater success. But as long as some platforms such as X, Telegram, and 4chan allow abusive material to proliferate at scale, the deluge will overwhelm even robust defenses.

In 2021, nine of the biggest tech companies formed a Digital Trust & Safety Partnership to improve risk detection and mitigation. However, companies remained highly resistant to experts' recommendations of third-party audits of their practices as well as the platforms' proprietary recommender algorithms and other trade secrets. Competitive pressures make it unlikely that a voluntary remedy will be adopted by for-profit corporations, suggesting that some form of regulation and oversight is needed for effective safety measures.

Despite growing calls for ethical AI and the need to consider the manifold risks up front when creating algorithms and designing and testing models, few companies have embraced and implemented safety-by-design principles. Indeed, there is ample evidence that the technology companies have extremely detailed knowledge of the harms and risks of their products but have proceeded with blatant disregard for them. A former Facebook employee, Frances Haugen, came forward in 2021 and testified to the U.S. Congress that the company was aware that its machine learning algorithms promoted hate speech, fake news, and death threats, but chose not to act—indeed, pay and bonuses were linked to increased engagements (or "clicks"), which the algorithms power.[33] She implored lawmakers to act, but no action was taken.

Leaked documents in a court case revealed that one of the most used video sharing platforms, TikTok, had studied in detail and recognized the severe harms its algorithms inflicted, in essence addicting users and causing mental and emotional pain.[34] And OpenAI, which was founded as a nonprofit aiming to develop safe and ethical AI, traded this mission for the all-out race to develop AI the fastest.[35] It released its generative AI program ChatGPT despite warnings of the dangers from the Association for the Advancement of Artificial Intelligence.

The tech world has earned a reputation for hostility to women, who are scarce in the tech world, especially at the top. Despite numerous lawsuits and companies' pledges to boost the hiring of women, the Equal Employment Opportunity Commission found that women's employment in the tech sector has remained essentially static.[36] Although women make up almost half of the total U.S. workforce, they held only 22.6 percent of the tech jobs in 2022, barely more than the 22 percent they held in 2005. Women tech entrepreneurs receive less than 2 percent of venture capital funding in the United States and Europe, and less than that elsewhere, according to Pitchbook data, despite rates of business success that outperform men two to one.[37]

The comments of several leading figures in the tech sector and its supporting venture capital industry have accentuated the industry's reputation as hostile to women and gender equality.[38] The most vocal figure is billionaire Elon Musk, who quickly readmitted misogynist influencers after purchasing Twitter, which he renamed X. He posted attacks on Harris and declared that "a Republic of high-status males is best for decision-making."[39] PayPal founder Peter Thiel, who funded JD Vance's entrance into politics, created waves with a 2009 essay, "The Education of a Libertarian." He wrote: "Since 1920, the vast increase in welfare beneficiaries and the extension of the franchise to women—two constituencies that are notoriously tough for libertarians—have rendered the notion of 'capitalist democracy' into an oxymoron."[40] Freedom and democracy, he concluded, are "no longer compatible."[41] Thiel, a gay man, also coauthored a book, *The Diversity Myth*, assailing diversity and multiculturalism in universities. At the same time that Meta CEO Zuckerberg ended third-party fact-checking for his social media platforms, he also ended DEI policies at his companies, stating that the corporate world was becoming "culturally neutered" and needed more "aggression" and "masculine energy."[42]

As the world's wealthiest individuals, leaders of the tech industry wield vast power not only through the increasing role of technology in daily life but also in shaping government policy and public opinion. The tech sector lobbied heavily against legislation in the U.S. Congress, along with free speech advocates and conservatives who believe the tech companies have censored their views disproportionately. Tech leaders have been joined by others who fear that regulation of artificial intelligence will create disadvantage in the global AI race, with dire economic and national security consequences.

FROM #NOTTHECOST TO WOMEN FIGHTING FOR SAFETY REGULATION

There is, however, a persistent and growing lobby in favor of tech regulation, which includes many women. The drive for safety legislation gained steam after deepfake images of Taylor Swift circled the globe in early 2024. Amid a surge of calls to regulate the industry and revise the 1996 Communication Decency Act, which shields companies from liability, tech leaders appeared before Congress and issued apologies to those harmed.[43] Several bills to criminalize sharing of deepfakes passed the Senate in 2024, though they died for lack of action in the Republican-controlled House.

Forty-eight states passed laws to criminalize nonconsensual image sharing of real images, though many have been contested. The 2022 reauthorization of the Violence Against Women Act allowed civil suits to be filed for unauthorized dissemination of intimate images. The law requires plaintiffs to prove the images were knowingly or recklessly shared, however, which is often impossible given the internet's anonymity and automatic propagation. The Cyber Civil Rights Initiative argues that statutes should focus instead on the harm caused, using the principle established in privacy law: "Similar to other privacy violations, whether the perpetrator intends to harm the victim-survivor or not is irrelevant to the magnitude of the harm caused."[44]

Madeleine Albright passed away in 2022, but the National Democratic Institute continued its campaign to curb violence against women in politics. It was dubbed #NotTheCost to rebut the common refrain that abuse and violence are just "the cost of doing politics" for women. The Trump administration cut funding for NDI and its parent organization, the National Endowment for Democracy, as part of its wholesale defunding and dismantling of programs to promote democracy and gender equality. A group of bipartisan legislators fought for some months to save NED, an organization started by Ronald Reagan, but failed to muster a majority as the administration pushed through new rounds of foreign aid cuts aimed at any programs addressing women, gender, or democracy. The John D. and Catherine T. MacArthur Foundation came forward with a grant to revive NDI for a year, raising hope that major philanthropies would fill the vacuum.

Women across the political spectrum have championed the need for digital safety, and many legislative proposals for online safety have bipartisan sponsorship. First Lady Melania Trump held a forum and threw her weight behind one of the proposals to criminalize deepfake porn, urging Congress to pass it. The Republican House leadership brought the bill to the floor, and the Take It Down Act passed in 2025 with bipartisan support. The first U.S. federal law to rein in deepfakes, the act criminalizes publication of nonconsensual intimate imagery and requires online platforms to remove the content within forty-eight hours of notice from the victim. The first lady subsequently spoke out for safety in AI development at the administration's first AI summit.

Women also stood up in a pivotal battle for digital safety that centered on the European Union's Digital Services Act. The law, which came into force in 2023, requires the largest tech companies to assess their platforms, apps, and services for six systemic risks, including gender-based violence, mitigate those risks, and provide documentation of their efforts or face penalties of up to 6 percent of gross revenues. The hefty fines—and the lucrative market of the world's second largest economy—had the potential to force companies to take responsibility for their products. When the Trump administration threatened to levy tariffs on the EU if it proceeded to enforce this law, European Commission President Ursula von der Leyen and other officials vowed to continue implementing the DSA as Europe's law of the land. In a speech at the Munich Security Conference, Vice President Vance called the EU commissioners "commissars" and called the EU's stand on digital safety the "enemy within." Other EU commissioners, which included a record number of women, also supported the need to enforce the DSA, as well as the EU Artificial Intelligence Act passed in 2024. The latter imposes similar safety requirements, including the testing of models for risk, the watermarking of deepfakes, and restrictions on the use of biometric and facial recognition programs. Von der Leyen emphasized that the EU supported digital innovation and investment but would do so while maintaining its commitment to digital safety. Just as Juana Quispe fought for the first law criminalizing violence against women in politics in Bolivia, women who face new digital forms of violence have the greatest incentive to pursue remedies and form alliances across party lines.

Chapter Four

THE ROLE MODEL EFFECT
OF WOMEN LEADERS

IN THE FACE OF SEXISM AND MISOGYNY, women have continued to fight for and win political power. Just as women have mobilized to demand adequate measures for digital safety, women politicians have continued run for and win top positions in government. As of late 2025, women led twenty-six countries. They were contributing to their democracies substantively and symbolically—a small wedge pressing into the rarefied male club of presidents and prime ministers, lending a pop of color in the lineup of suits at multilateral leadership gatherings. Their presence makes democracy more representative, yet they are more than tokens. Not only have they fought for and won their offices, but their acts of governance rebut the claim that women are not capable of leading countries. Their examples create powerful knock-on effects as their governing reduces bias, increases support, and encourages other women to enter the ring.

Not all women leaders are successful, and some of them are undemocratic. But they prove that politics is not just a man's business and executive leadership skills are not inherently masculine. This stereotype is grounded in a view that only men possess the traits of decisiveness, firmness, and strength to do the job of leading countries, a centralized and hierarchical function that marries politics, power, and military command.[1] Male candidates tend to reinforce this stereotype through displays of strength, dominance, and affiliation with the military. By contrast, women candidates who display supposedly "masculine" traits and expertise are subjected to criticism for stepping out of their expected gender roles, a phenomenon known as the double bind.

According to the World Values Survey, which represents 85 percent of the global population, 49 percent of respondents believe that men make better leaders of countries.[2] The other half (51 percent) is open to women as leaders. The math is complicated by the calculations of voters who are not biased but do not want to waste their votes on a losing candidate. This strategic or pragmatic bias is substantial: A majority (65 percent) of Americans believe that U.S. voters are more likely to vote for a white male candidate, according to a 2023 Pew survey.[3]

EVIDENCE THAT WOMEN CAN GOVERN CHIPS AWAY AT BIAS

The good news is that while gender bias may still be prevalent, it is not immutable. Research shows that, over the past decade, the masculine stereotype has been eroding as more people have seen women leaders in action. They now credit women with being more powerful, having more capabilities, and possessing higher general competence that they previously thought, while also retaining favorable traits attributed to females such as empathy and integrity.[4] The "role model effect" works in three ways: It reduces the bias, increases public support for women politicians, and encourages more women to get into politics.[5] While women's gains in politics have provoked backlash in some quarters, the 2023 Gender Social Norms Index report found "overwhelming evidence" that women's growing visibility and representation "can be powerful inspirations for change."[6]

This conclusion has been backed up by other evidence. An Ipsos poll of thirty-six countries found that the experience of having a woman leader made voters more disposed to consider either a man or a woman candidate.[7] In the United States, having a woman governor at the state level increased voters' willingness to vote for a woman presidential candidate.[8] And voters' concerns about a woman candidate's electability could be altered, a study found, by presenting evidence that women earn as much electoral support as men in U.S. general elections.[9]

Africa has also seen growing acceptance of women in politics. In twenty-one countries where the number of women politicians has increased over the past decade, support has increased markedly for the idea that women should have the same chance of being elected to political office as men.[10] Support also increased in another six African countries even though the actual number of women politicians did not grow.

A review of public opinion polls conducted in forty countries between 2010 and 2014 found that women leaders positively affected views about women in politics and made women more likely to engage in politics.[11] Eighty-two countries that have had a woman president or prime minister have either reelected those women or elected other women leaders, suggesting that once the barrier is broken a bandwagon effect can occur. And even with the headwinds women have faced in the past decade, more than a dozen countries have selected their first women heads of state or government and reelected a number of those women. Aspiring candidates also gained concrete help from women leaders' insights into paths to power and ways to overcame obstacles.[12]

CHANGING VIEWS OF WOMEN'S COMPETENCE IN FOREIGN AFFAIRS

Women are now much more likely to be seen as possessing essential traits for leadership. A 2023 Pew poll of U.S. voters found that 68 percent of respondents believed men and women were equally qualified in a range of relevant leadership skills, including the ability to compromise, engage respectfully, be honest and ethical, maintain firmly held beliefs, and handle pressure.[13] However, 46 percent still believed that the country was not ready to elect a woman president—a sign of strategic bias or hidden bias that could significantly alter actual voting behavior. Also, 31 percent of Republicans believed that a woman president would be less respected globally.

On specific areas of competence, some distinctions still exist. A significant minority still see men as more capable in the domains of national security and defense by, while women tend to be seen as better in areas of domestic policy such as health and education. The view that women are less competent in national security and foreign policy and less able to perform the role of commander in chief constitutes a significant vulnerability for women seeking to lead countries because these are core functions of the chief executive, who wields the power to take the nation to war. In the Ipsos poll, twice as many respondents said that men were more capable in national security, and a U.S. poll found that 37 percent believed men were better at dealing with national security and defense.[14]

If the role model theory is correct, doubts about women's competence in the areas of national security and foreign policy may diminish further as the evidence becomes increasingly robust. In her book *Women as Foreign Policy Leaders*, Sylvia Bashevkin documented how both Republican and Democratic secretaries of state made a measurable difference in national security policy and pursued muscular foreign policies.[15] In addition to the 174 women who have served as elected heads of state and government, the ranks of women at senior levels of national security establishments have grown significantly in recent years. More than a hundred women have served as ministers of defense in dozens of countries, including Chile, Germany, and Canada. President Biden appointed women to lead the navy and the coast guard and to serve as secretary of the army, head of national intelligence, and deputy secretary of defense, though not Michèle Flournoy, as many expected, to the post of secretary of defense.

Women have also contributed to theoretical advances in understanding the complex sources of insecurity and developing strategies to address them. Of particular importance in the current era is understanding that addressing security threats involves far more than arraying armies and tanks to repel military invasions, as competition and conflict occur across cyber, information, economic, and political dimensions. Deterrence, diplomacy, risk assessment, and conflict management are just as important as fighting wars. Women leaders have gained firsthand experience in countering hybrid warfare waged by Russia, China, and other aggressors that aim to destabilize or overthrow their governments. Women leaders have also been instrumental in building movements and coalitions to defend democracy.

Women are playing leading roles in addressing systemic threats that now top the global agenda, including the existential challenge of climate change, as well as pandemics, mass migration, and cyber threats that have enormous capacity to destabilize societies. Women leaders in Taiwan, New Zealand, Finland, and elsewhere were credited with containing the pandemic with minimal loss of life with science-based policies. Prime Minister Mia Amor Mottley of Barbados achieved major financial reforms to enable developing countries to cope with escalating climate disasters. She and other women leaders such as Slovenia's Nataša Pirc Musar have also pressed for reform of global institutions like the United Nations to make them more representative and more effective in addressing a record number of global conflicts and refugees.

While women have gained experience at the cabinet level, they are still far more likely to be appointed to "soft" ministries rather than the power positions of defense, foreign affairs, and finance, where men still hold more than 80 percent of the cabinet posts. The United States achieved parity in cabinet appointments for the first time during the Biden administration, when women served as secretaries of treasury, commerce, and interior as well as head of national intelligence, trade, and other agencies. Women have also achieved notable success at the head of international financial institutions, with Christine Lagarde leading the International Monetary Fund and the European Central Bank, Kristalina Georgieva succeeding Lagarde at the IMF, and Ngozi Okonjo-Iweala leading the World Trade Organization.

In the realm of domestic policy, women's competence is more widely accepted.[16] Women legislators have been active and effective in domestic policy and climate policy, and at least some of these findings may translate to the national executive leader level. Women legislators tend to advocate for increased spending and legislation on health, education, welfare, and gender equality. Women have achieved both legislation and policy outcomes when they reach a critical mass of 30 percent or more in legislatures. Their focus on domestic policy has been attributed to socialization such as family roles that make them more aware of the benefits to overall well-being, including a country's GDP.[17]

Many women leaders have also been attuned to the connection between democratic resilience and policies that meet the needs of population subgroups including youth, the elderly, and marginalized people. They have been supportive of measures to address the mental health effects of social media usage, disinformation, social polarization, disinformation, and other internal vulnerabilities that adversaries routinely exploit to weaken countries and gain advantage. While women fall on both sides of the gender equality culture wars, they may be best positioned to support families and help forge a consensus in areas that require public policy responses. Women's negotiation skills have been shown by their successes in reaching legislative compromises as well as more enduring and successful peace accords in cases of interstate and intrastate conflict. For example, accords are 35 percent likelier to last fifteen years or more if women are at the negotiating table.[18]

KAMALA HARRIS IN THE 2024 PRESIDENTIAL RACE

The presidential campaign of Kamala Harris as the first Black and South Asian woman nominated for the U.S. presidency provides an important example of a women leader surmounting enormous hurdles to close within a hair of victory. She had already broken barriers in previous elections to become district attorney and attorney general of California, the first Black and South Asian woman U.S. senator from California, and the first female U.S. vice president. Harris ran a strong campaign despite a last-minute candidacy when Joe Biden withdrew from the race. She campaigned energetically with a positive message, made eloquent appeals to unity, and put forward detailed proposals to address voters' pressing daily needs. Polls showed she was popular; she raised a billion dollars and filled stadiums with enthusiastic supporters. She was widely seen as the winner of the only debate that Trump agreed to. In the end, Harris lost by just 1.5 percentage points, winning 48.3 percent of the votes to Trump's 49.8 percent. Given that she had only 107 days to make her case, it was an impressive result.

These results were even more impressive given the sexist and racist attacks that exceeded the high levels she had surmounted over the course of her career. Bias surfaced in other ways: During her three and a half years as vice president, her substantial work in the areas of space, artificial intelligence, gender, overseas diplomacy, and regional issues of trade and development remained largely unrecognized.[19] Harris revived the race; her results halved the 3 percent gap between Trump and Biden when the latter left the race in July 2024. Her Hail Mary candidacy met the definition of the "glass cliff" phenomenon, in which women are put forward in times of crisis. Going forward, the risk was that her loss, following Clinton's loss in 2016, would create reluctance to nominate a woman again. That would be a mistake, however, as the record shows that Harris provided a positive role model and achieved creditable results in unfavorable circumstances.

ENCOURAGEMENT FOR WOMEN CANDIDATES

The collective example of women's leadership in the Nordic countries and their pathway to achieving power have led many countries to follow suit in adopting policies that lessen the obstacles for women's ability to compete for power. The Nordic region leads the world in women's political leadership, with repeated elections of women to the highest office and near parity in many of its parliaments. Most of the Nordic countries have adopted policies to overcome the structural barriers that women traditionally face in the workplace, including competing for and holding office. Generous government support for childcare, health care, and parental leave, as well as equal pay and equal opportunity laws, make it possible for parents to share the collective functions of family, work, and governance.

Nordic countries have not only served as a model but actively aided other countries through their foreign policies and assistance as well as through international organizations. The European Union followed the Nordic example in adopting gender equality standards as part of its governing statutes for member states and requirements for new members. In 2003, Norway was the first country to pass a law requiring that women occupy at least 40 percent of board seats of publicly held companies.[20] The EU adopted that standard for publicly listed companies with more than 250 employees, as well as a goal to achieve gender parity in EU leadership and management positions.

The Nordic countries have not been exempted from the right-wing authoritarian, anti-immigrant, and violent extremist trends chronicled in this book. Far-right parties have sprung up in Finland and elsewhere. Sweden's conservative government has stepped back from its predecessor's first ever feminist foreign policy, though it has said it continues to support gender equality objectives. Nordic countries still score at the top of most gender equality indices, and Sweden scores 82 out of 100 in the EU Gender Equality Index, compared to an average score of 71.

Gender quotas can also increase public support for women in politics. The most effective type of quota for generating both representation and positive views of women in politics appears to be providing competitive slots for women candidates with measures that enable them to compete equally (for example, alternating positions on party lists). A study found that such quotas for candidates increased approval of women in politics by up to 38.6 percent.[21] In parliamentary systems of government, women's gains in the legislature can lead directly to leadership positions in cabinets or as prime minister candidates.[22] Women's roles in cabinet positions have also shown to increase women's political engagement.[23]

THE DIVERSITY OF WOMEN LEADERS

Increasingly, women are successfully adopting a mix of leadership styles as the masculine stereotype breaks down. Women are freer to adopt the blend of agentic and communal traits and approaches that suits them and resonates with their constituents.[24] They are less likely to be caught in the so-called double bind in which women politicians are traditionally punished by lower favorability ratings if they display the agentic traits seen as required for leadership: decisiveness, firmness, aggressiveness. Women leaders like Danish Prime Minister Mette

Frederiksen have developed a style that is authentic, assertive, and even dominant. Frederiksen has been successful, winning reelection in 2022 after her first election in 2019.

Her path was blazed by Helle Thorning-Schmidt, Denmark's first woman prime minister from 2011 to 2015, who encountered significant sexism, as recounted in a documentary she made in 2024. Both Danish leaders made waves, each in her own way. Frederiksen pulled the liberal Social Democratic Party to the right to address Danish concerns about being overwhelmed by immigration with sometimes controversial policies to restrict numbers of entrants and to foster linguistic and cultural integration. But Thorning-Schmidt also pushed back against the right-wing populist trend of anti–gender equality policies; she and her transgender child have spoken out in efforts to bridges divides, increase public understanding, and reduce the demonization of transgender people. And on defense, among European leaders, Frederiksen has been one of the foremost proponents of aid to Ukraine, giving Denmark's F-16 fighter jets to help Ukraine defend itself from Russia's invasion and boosting aid well beyond that of most West European countries on a GNP per capita basis.

Women still struggle with the straitjacket that their gender imposes in other ways. As with all politicians, their positions vary, as do their policy priorities; they adapt as they encounter new facts or new conditions, or as pragmatic adjustments to maintain support and stay in power. Gender does not need to determine their positions, yet too often women labor against the presumption that their decisions must flow primarily from their identity as women. To be seen always as first a woman is a corrosive form of sexism that causes their messages to be lost, their impact lessened, and their achievements overlooked.

Women leaders chafe at these myriad shackles. Judging from those I've met, they want above all to be seen and evaluated as leaders, plain and simple. Seeking to avoid being pigeonholed, Frederiksen turned to me before we went on stage for a moderated talk and said, "Please don't ask me any 'woman' questions." Despite our preparatory work, she remained concerned that I might go down that road, even though my background is foreign policy and not gender studies. The comment drove home to me how easily women can be straitjacketed by someone bringing attention to their gender, and how sensitive even the most accomplished and long-serving leaders are to the risk of their message being derailed by awakening concerns about them as women. Her sensitivity may have been heightened by the fact that she had just been attacked by an assailant on the streets of Copenhagen. While she had been rightly shaken and furious at the assault on the office of the prime minister as much as on her person, she did not want to get into that at a crucial moment for Western foreign policy.

Frederiksen was in Washington for the NATO summit, where the issues of Russia's attacks and European and Ukrainian responses had come to a head. As one of Europe's stalwart allies and one of the most active donors to Ukraine's defense, the prime minister needed her message, not her person, to be the sole focus. Indeed, as a forceful speaker, she was resoundingly clear: Aid to Ukraine was being delivered too slowly, with too many constraints, and its war effort was faltering. Moreover, Russia had begun conducting sabotage and hybrid attacks directly in NATO countries, and a response was needed.[25] The West needed to move further and faster, in her assessment, and she had come to spur NATO—most of all President Biden—to more urgent collective action as Putin was ramping up attacks inside Ukraine and, alarmingly, in sabotage attacks across Europe.

WOMEN CAN ALSO BE AUTHORITARIANS

Women are not necessarily democratic. They are subject to the same social and political influences as men, and they prioritize issues that they deem most important. Some even disagree that women should have the same rights as men. Women leaders are found on both sides of the democrat-authoritarian divide, and many women vote for authoritarian leaders. Some regions, such as Asia, have produced a significant number of women authoritarian leaders, possibly because of their dynastic path to power. Also, authoritarians have appointed women to positions of relative power, or at least visibility. Trump appointed women cabinet members to carry out the purge of the intelligence community, the weaponization of the justice department, and the dismantling of the education department.

The histories, words, and deeds of women who are authoritarians or would-be authoritarians provide insight into their ideological motivations as well as factors that cause them to moderate or change course. The rising right-wing populism of

Europe features several prominent examples of women leaders, among them France's Marine Le Pen, Germany's Alice Weidel, and Italy's Giorgia Meloni, who are positioned to shape their countries and Europe's right-wing trend. They were not authoritarians as of 2025, but many of their policies or policy proposals were exclusionary and restrictive of rights, raising questions about their commitment to democratic norms. They advocate anti-immigrant, anti-Muslim policies, and anti–gender equality policies with discriminatory ethnonationalist implications.

Marine Le Pen took up her father's mantle as leader of France's far-right party, the National Front (now called the National Rally), and even though she was banned from running for president in 2027, her party remains the dominant right-wing party in France. She moved the party in a more moderate direction, away from her father's anti-Semitism, as she sought to broaden the party's base, but anti-immigrant, anti-Muslim, and ethnonationalist policies remain the party's central planks. The proposals, if implemented, would discriminate against many French citizens, deny them services, and entail the use of state power and sanctions to enforce them. The party has also supported Russia in numerous ways.

Alice Weidel is cochair of the Alternative for Germany party (AfD), which achieved a historic second place in the country's 2025 elections. The German domestic intelligence service has deemed some elements of the party extremist, and some leaders have been sanctioned for using banned Nazi slogans. Weidel is an unusual figure for the anti-immigrant, anti-Muslim, far-right party in that she is a lesbian with a Sri

Lankan–born partner and two adopted sons. But Weidel, whose grandfather was a Nazi judge, staunchly supports the party's promotion of anti–gender equality policies and mass deportation of even legal immigrants. Other women leaders have played important supporting roles to authoritarian populists, including Ana Brnabić, also a lesbian, who served as prime minister alongside the right-wing Serbian President Aleksandar Vučić.

EUROPE'S LEADING RIGHT-WING POPULIST IS A WOMAN

The most powerful woman leader in Europe's right-wing populist movement is Giorgia Meloni, Italy's first woman prime minister. First elected to parliament in 2005, Meloni joined the neofascist Italian Social Movement as a youth. She split with Silvio Berlusconi in 2012 to form her own party, the Brothers of Italy, which won the most votes with 26 percent in the 2022 elections. Meloni formed Italy's first majority government in years with two other right-wing populist parties. Forbes named her the third most powerful woman in the world in its 2024 rankings, and Politico ranked her as the most powerful person in Europe in 2025.

Meloni summed up her firebrand politics at a rally in 2022: "Yes to the natural family, no to the LGBT lobby, yes to sexual identity, no to gender ideology. No to Islamist violence, yes to secure borders. No to mass migration, no to big international finance, no to the bureaucrats of Brussels." She embraced the

Great Replacement theory that immigrants and leftist politics are threatening Italy's national identity as a white, Christian, European country, writing in her biography, *I Am Giorgia*, "Does this make me an ignorant xenophobe or a bigot?"[26] After courts stymied her plan to enact processing of migrants' asylum claims at an offshore center in Albania, she turned to other less controversial measures, with EU support, to persuade North African states to step up border controls and also launched state investments in Africa.

Meloni has tacked to the center on foreign policy. She had previously railed against the European Union and the euro as Italy's currency, but as prime minister she needed to ensure the continued flow of much-needed EU funds to the heavily indebted country.[27] Meloni was aligned with the EU in other ways: She strongly criticized Russia's invasion of Ukraine and used her influence to persuade Orbán not to block the EU's fund for Ukraine. She also proposed a NATO-like Article V security guarantee for Ukraine and helped promote it to President Trump.

On the domestic front, Meloni kept to her populist platform. On gender rights, she did not seek to overturn the 1978 law legalizing abortion or the civil union law but has sought to discourage abortion and opposes same-sex marriage. Her government also passed laws allowing only biological parents to be listed on birth certificates and banning Italians from seeking surrogacy abroad. Despite her embrace of Christianity and the traditional family, she had a child out of wedlock and remains unmarried. Being a right-wing icon has not protected Meloni from sexist attack, however. She fought back when she was victimized by deepfake porn, which was posted to an American website and seen by millions of viewers. She sued the perpetrators, pledged the proceeds to domestic violence survivors, and vowed to push for stiffer laws against deepfake porn.[28] As online attacks continued, she denounced websites that posted thousands of manipulated images and videos of her and other women, often accompanied by obscene and violent commentary. Meloni said, "It is disheartening to see that in 2025, there are still those who consider it normal and legitimate to trample on a woman's dignity and make her the object of sexist and vulgar insults, hiding behind anonymity or a keyboard."[29]

Meloni describes herself as a conservative and denies that she is far-right. However, as prime minister she took several actions that called into question her commitment to liberal democratic norms. Unauthorized protests have been criminalized, journalists threatened and harassed, and judicial reforms instituted that could make prosecutors more susceptible to political influence.[30] Meloni also proposed changing Italy's electoral law to give the party winning an election with a minority share of votes an automatic majority in parliament, similar to a reform that helped Orbán solidify his control in Hungary.

Meloni's pragmatism, and the economic incentive to steer clear of EU sanctions, may prevent Italy from following Hungary's path to competitive authoritarianism. However, there is no doubt that she is a right-wing populist, as well as an astute politician and communicator, who has become a leading voice of today's conservatism. She served as an avenue for cooperation between European governments and the Trump administration. Speaking by video link to the Conservative Political Action Conference shortly after Trump's inauguration, she underlined the importance of U.S.-European ties and the ideological bond as she saw it: "The political battle for the values of US conservatives is not only fought in the US. It is a battle of the western world: I still believe in the western world not only in geographical boundaries but as a civilization."

WOMEN LEADERS ACROSS THE POLITICAL SPECTRUM

Meloni has challenged democratic norms in ways that raise questions about whether she may cross the line into authoritarianism. But there is no doubt that she has broken through presumptions that only men can lead Italy with a commanding governing style, competence in pursuing her policy agenda, and her robust response to gender-based attacks. She outmaneuvered her mentor Silvio Berlusconi, who sought to undercut her with sexist attacks as she vied for leadership of the fractured Italian right. She presided over the longest-serving government in the country's recent history, asserted her leadership among her coalition partners, and maintained her base of support despite the chaotic nature of Italian politics in a country deeply divided between right and left. Meloni tapped into a conservative, Catholic, white Italian base and secured the approval of one-third of the electorate as of late 2025.

There are other women leaders who are breaking the stereotype that only men can lead countries and who are also on the borderline of authoritarianism. In Africa, Tanzania's Samia Suluhu Hassan, following the disastrous and bloody elections of 2025, may continue on that road rather than returning to her early path of liberalizing the political climate. She may opt for strengthening the country's growing relationship with China as some in the United States call for reevaluating the long-standing support to the country through foreign aid, including democracy and gender equality programs. Mexico's first woman president, Claudia Sheinbaum, showed high competence in her first year of leadership, winning high marks for fending off punitive tariffs and threats of military incursion by President Trump. She projected calm authority, avoiding antagonistic clashes, but made no compromises to Mexican sovereignty. However, she came to power in an increasingly undemocratic system that her party and predecessor created, and it is not clear whether she will continue that trend or adopt a more liberal path.

The following chapters examine the path to power and the governing records of six women leaders in Taiwan, Moldova, Estonia, Kosovo, Slovenia, and Barbados. These in-depth profiles represent a diverse sample in geography, from Asia to Europe to the Western Hemisphere, and political ideologies, political systems, and personal characteristics such as race and marital status. While the preponderance of women leaders continues to be in Europe, the subregional contexts and challenges differ greatly in the Baltics, the Balkans, and Eastern Europe compared to Meloni in Western Europe, where migration has sparked the most intense xenophobic reactions. In Africa and the Middle East, women have too rarely made it to positions of real power. Their political ideologies notably range from right and center-right to center-left, independent, and progressive, and they have governed in both presidential and parliamentary democracies. These countries include relatively new democracies and democracies in transition, which as Farida Jalalzai's work has demonstrated, have typically provided greater opportunities for women to compete for power.[31]

Countries were also selected for the presence of a significant and even existential crisis with foreign policy or national security ramifications. This provided the opportunity to examine in detail how women leaders have governed under circumstances of duress, challenging the propositions that only men can lead countries and that women are less capable in matters of international affairs. Taiwan's President Tsai Ing-wen faced China's saber-rattling, Moldova's Maia Sandu confronted Russian hybrid warfare, and Estonia's Kaja Kallas confronted Russia's threat to Estonia and the rest of Europe when she became EU chief of foreign policy and defense. Women presidents Vjosa Osmani and Nataša Pirc Musar in the restive Western Balkans governed amid regional conflict and internal strife that threatened their democracies. Barbados's Mia Amor Mottley took on climate and debt crises that pose acute threats to the Caribbean and much of the Global South. All faced persistent sexism.

The task of addressing the acute global threats of authoritarian aggression, democratic backsliding, and climate change was further complicated by the fact that they led small countries, requiring them to employ a variety of strategies rather than raw power. Taiwan, Moldova, and Estonia are frontline targets of the world's two major authoritarian powers, China and Russia. Both adversaries employ forms of hybrid warfare that use not only military might but also political, economic, informational, and cyber tactics that exploit domestic vulnerabilities including corruption and polarization. This set a high bar for the leaders' capabilities in both foreign and domestic policy.

The two women presidents Osmani and Pirc Musar faced internal and external conflicts in the Western Balkans, Europe's most unstable region, but also the limitations of governing alongside prime ministers in dual-executive political systems. Both countries encountered hostility from an authoritarian neighbor, Serbia, backed by Russia, which is a major destabilizing force in the region and particularly in Kosovo, which it refuses to recognize. Slovenia suffered a severe democratic regression with a pro-Trump right-wing populist leader who was ousted following a mass protest, as well as spillover effects of the long-running Balkans tensions. These countries' paths were further complicated by the stalled integration of the Western Balkans into the European Union, as Europe has been preoccupied with Russia, and loss of assistance and support from the United States.

Not all existential challenges are posed by states. The dangers that climate change and debt pose to Barbados and the rest of the developing world, and the reluctance of global financial powers to address either, are rightly seen as national security and human security threats. The Caribbean island's first woman prime minister, Mia Amor Mottley, faced this dual crisis from her first days in office and negotiated with banks and world leaders to secure new solutions for financing and climate adaptation. She and the other leaders addressed significant attacks for their gender from both internal and external sources, with the aim of discrediting and derailing their governance, by pursuing greater gender equality and fighting back in other ways.

The accounts of their leadership explore five areas: their experience in being targeted by sexist attacks; their responses to authoritarianism and other existential challenges at home and abroad; their records in defending and promoting democracy; their actions to support gender equality and remedy other social injustice; and the degree to which being a woman affected their governing approach, successes, and setbacks. Their stories and those of the women in earlier chapters show diverse women leading in circumstances that test their competence in governing, their capacity to conduct international affairs, and their potential demonstration effects and impact on future women leaders.

Chapter Five

TSAI ING-WEN

CONFRONTING CHINA'S AGGRESSION
AGAINST TAIWAN

TAIWAN'S FIRST FEMALE PRESIDENT, Tsai Ing-wen, governed from 2016 to 2024 amid historic tensions with an increasingly bellicose China, which claims the mountainous island eighty-one miles from the mainland. Tsai broke barriers not only in Taiwan but in all of Asia as the first woman president to be elected without family ties to politics. During her tenure, Tsai kept China at bay by shoring up the island's defenses and its ties abroad while repairing its social safety net at home and expanding gender equality and support for its indigenous populations. She did so amid persistent sexist attacks from her political rivals and as part of China's continuous hybrid warfare campaign.

Governing Taiwan is a daunting challenge given the country's unusual circumstances. Chinese pressure has led most countries to withdraw formal diplomatic recognition from Taiwan, though it maintains informal relations abroad through more than a hundred cultural and trade offices. The United States does not recognize China's claim over Taiwan, which relies heavily on U.S. defense sales to the island. While it possesses all the features of a country—a currency, government institutions, schools and social services, defense forces, and a thriving economy and trade as the world's top maker of advanced semiconductors—Taiwan navigates a gray world in diplomatic terms amid relentless military, cyber, and disinformation attacks from China.

A lawyer by training, Tsai found her way into government through her trade expertise and was then recruited into politics. "A political career wasn't, you know, anything planned by myself or my parents," she said, commenting on her accidental career.[1] After earning advanced law degrees at Cornell Law School in New York and the London School of Economics, Tsai became the chief legal adviser to Taiwan's government in trade talks with the United States and then negotiations to join the World Trade Organization (WTO). Joining the WTO in 2011 marked a diplomatic and commercial breakthrough for Taiwan, which holds member status in forty multilateral organizations.

Taiwan's President Lee Teng-hui asked Tsai to advise him and the National Security Council to help prepare a plan for cross-strait talks with China. "I learned a lot from the [trade] process, especially when you're negotiating from a weaker party's position," Tsai reflected. "Given the political situation we are in, also we sometimes feel . . . we don't have that much political leverage." Her skill led the next president, Chen Shui-bian, to appoint her chair of the Mainland Affairs

Council in 2000, when the Democratic Progressive Party (DPP) won its first elections, ending a half-century of Kuomintang (KMT) rule. Tsai served as minister for four years, gaining national visibility as she negotiated transit and business links with China. She overcame her shyness and the pressure of being grilled by the legislature for hours on national television. "Somehow, I became a bit popular among the public here, because of the way I responded to questions in the legislature," she said. "People found it interesting because they were not a traditional type of pure political answers."

In 2004, Tsai accepted the DPP's invitation to join the party and was elected to an at-large seat in parliament, thus making the transition from technocrat to politician. President Chen was voted out in 2008 after he became embroiled in corruption scandals. Some party leaders suggested that Tsai, as a woman, could help recover the party's fortunes, but others argued that the Taiwanese would not elect a woman as leader of the country. Tsai won the vote to become party chair, but she continued to be confronted with sexism as she ascended the political ladder. Tsai, a political novice, also suffered early defeats. She lost a bid to become mayor of New Taipei City; while she had formulated detailed proposals to improve the major city's services, she had not connected with voters on a human level. "I was talking to them like a professor," she confessed. Over time, Tsai became more comfortable campaigning and on social media, where she shared her life with her beloved cats Think Think and Ah Tsai, who also wandered into her video chats and interviews.

LEARNING FROM LOSSES

Tsai faced blatant sexism from her competitors and even her party leadership when she ran for president in 2012. "A skirt-wearer is unfit to be a commander in chief," one DPP leader said. Tsai lost the race to the incumbent KMT president Ma Ying-jeou, but Tsai said more than sexism was to blame. "It would take me another four years to convince the public in Taiwan that I would manage the cross-strait relationship in a very careful manner," Tsai said. The Obama administration harbored doubts as well: A U.S. official told the press that "she left us with distinct doubts about whether she is both willing and able to continue the stability in cross-Strait relations the region has enjoyed in recent years."[2]

Tsai ran again in 2016, facing sexism once again from party rivals, opposition candidates, and China, where Xi Jinping had cultivated a macho image with the nickname Big Daddy Xi. But other factors helped Tsai. U.S. concerns over China grew as Xi's policy become more aggressive, with outright threats to Taiwan, an island-building effort in the South China Sea, and a massive military buildup. Taiwan was also changing. Two-thirds of Taiwan's population now saw themselves as exclusively Taiwanese rather than Chinese, compared to 17.6 percent who held that view in 1992.[3] As their sense of national identity grew, Taiwanese began to question the KMT's approach to China favoring unification under its own version of a "one country, two systems" policy that left open just what that one China looked like and how it would be achieved. More people came to see unification on Beijing's terms as undesirable and unachievable on Taiwan's terms. Only 10 percent of Taiwanese supported unification with China; the majority placed a higher priority on maintaining their hard-won democracy and freedom.

Tsai's bid was aided by growing skepticism of the KMT as well as support from young Taiwanese. After the KMT government tried to steamroller legislative approval of its Cross-Strait Service Trade Agreement with China, the Sunflower Movement erupted with a twenty-four-day sit-in that attracted hundreds of thousands of protestors.[4] Tsai supported the protest, adding that she would not provoke a crisis with China. She had learned from her defeat in 2012 that above all she must be seen as a steady hand.

Tsai carefully calibrated her positions on China. She rejected Beijing's "one country, two systems" formula in which Taiwan was a province of China, but she pledged not to make any unilateral moves to change the status quo and to maintain the stability needed for economic development. She insisted that cross-strait relations "would be managed in a democratic way, meaning that the future of Taiwan is actually to be decided by the people of Taiwan." That was for many Taiwanese the critical difference between her and President Ma, who seemed too eager to compromise with China.

WINNING DESPITE SEXISM

Tsai won a landslide with 56 percent of the vote, as the party gained a majority of seats in the legislature for the first time ever, as well as 72 percent of local municipalities. Tsai launched an ambitious effort to address the country's many domestic problems, which ranged from a nearly bankrupt pension system to aging and inadequate infrastructure, insufficient water, electricity, and pollution control. Her pension and labor reforms sparked protests and controversy, but Tsai was resolute, saying "If you ask me to sit there and do nothing, I might as well not be president."

Alongside her effort to improve the situation for everyone, Tsai sought to fulfill her pledge to legalize same-sex marriage, but conservative and religious groups succeeded in passing a referendum restricting marriage to the union between a man and a woman. The DPP lost badly in the 2018 local elections, and Tsai resigned her post as party chair while continuing her to serve her term as president. "That was a difficult time for me," she recalled, as both her economic and social agenda faltered, and with it her approval ratings. Tsai would not give up on gender equality, however, and in 2019 brought the measure forward again. Young Taiwanese mobilized to ensure its passage, and Tsai acknowledged their weight in shifting the balance of public opinion. "What is most important is that while we are going through all these changes, it is the young people who are doing the change," she said. "The young people in Taiwan are invaluable assets to Taiwan's democracy."

As the 2020 elections approached, senior party leaders did not want her to run, and her premier Lai Ching-te challenged her for the nomination. Tsai won the primary and invited Lai to be her running mate. Tsai had faced gendered attacks in every race she ran, confronting sexism from rival politicians and as a main theme in China's disinformation campaign. Her status as a single woman with no children was a major theme. "She isn't qualified to talk about the next generation, because she doesn't have children of her own," said rival politician Yang Shih-kuang. The KMT party chair called her "an ill-starred woman," and another politician criticized her as unfit because she had never given birth. "I find such a political culture unacceptable, and we will not accept any personal attacks against women using such language," Tsai replied on social media.[5]

Sexism attacks also featured centrally in China's unrelenting propaganda campaign that bombarded Tsai with false accusations and relentless sexist innuendo and defamation of her as an unmarried woman. A three-hundred-page ebook, *The Secret History of Tsai Ing-wen*, attributed to China, alleged that she made her career through sexual promiscuity.[6] The book was designed to become an automated source of memes and narratives, and it predictably spawned a deluge of deepfakes that were propagated across Instagram, TikTok, and YouTube.

Sexist Chinese propaganda was compounded by attacks from her competitors in the 2019 campaign, which commentators judged to exceed the sexist attacks from other quarters, amplified by technology.[7] Rather than ignore the barrage, Tsai again defended herself and directly rebuked her main opponent, Han Kuo-yo, during a televised debate on behalf of all women. Tsai was threatened physically as well, in one case with beheading, an online threat for which the perpetrator was arrested.

Among the sexist remarks, Tsai's childless status became an issue, with candidates again claiming that she did not understand family needs. Tsai pushed back in a Facebook post, fully responding to the allegation on behalf of herself, her record, and all women without children. She called out the nonstop abuse she had sustained and defended her long record of supporting family policies. She wrote:

> Since I entered politics, these sorts of personal attacks against me have never stopped. Many Taiwanese women also frequently experience this sort of treatment. In the past three years since I came to office, we've increased basic salaries, reduced taxes for families, widened subsidies for childcare, build social housing, and promoted elderly care policies. . . . Launching personal attacks on the basis of gender or fertility status is an act that negates women and undermines the efforts of the government. Many young parents in Taiwan are working hard for the next generation, but there are also people who haven't married and had kids. This doesn't mean that they can't empathize with the hardships of being a parent.[8]

Han's comments, as well as derogatory comments about Tsai by his running mate, party chair, and the KMT mayor of Taipei, created a wave of criticism against the KMT for sexist and racist attitudes, which may have helped Tsai's victory. However, China's crackdown on the protest movement in Hong Kong made defense of democracy the pivotal issue In Taiwan's elections. The brutal repression and the passage of draconian national security laws in Hong Kong pushed more people to vote for her as the staunchest candidate opposing

China. Xi Jinping tried to force Tsai's hand during the campaign with an open letter demanding that she endorse the "one country, two systems" formula for Taiwan, and she refused. Upping the ante, Xi announced in a speech that unification was "inevitable," leading Tsai to reply that Taiwan would never give up its democratic freedoms.

Tsai won reelection in 2020 in a landslide with 57 percent of the vote and the most votes any candidate had ever received. "China's actions changed people's perception entirely," she said, and "made them very nervous about the intentions of the Chinese authorities." Many Hongkongers fled to Taiwan and bolstered the determination of many Taiwanese to defend their own democracy. With the world now riveted on one of the tensest corners in the world, *Time* magazine named Tsai to its list of the one hundred most influential people.

TSAI'S THREE-PRONGED STRATEGY TO DEFEND TAIWAN

"People loved to label DPP as a troublemaker in the cross-strait relations," she said, but after four years of carefully managing the relationship, "the label of troublemaker was gradually taken away." China was instead seen as the troublemaker through its behavior and steadily increasing pressure on the island, sending dozens and sometimes hundreds of military aircraft into Taiwan's air defense zone every day and staging frequent maritime incursions and air-sea military exercises in the Taiwan Strait.[9] Given these provocations, Taiwan's efforts to bolster its defenses and increase its resilience appeared to be a reasonable and necessary response.

Tsai launched initiatives to strengthen Taiwan's defense capacity under a new strategy to counter China's use of asymmetric warfare, including disinformation, cyber, and high-tech military power. Taiwan developed both government and nonprofit organizations skilled at rapidly detecting and responding to China's constant cognitive warfare. Over her tenure in office, Tsai almost doubled defense spending to 2.6 percent of GDP, increased Taiwan's military reserves to 1.66 million, and expanded its defense industrial capacity to build ships, submarines, and jet trainers. Taiwan extended its mandatory military service to one year and created a civil defense force to provide first aid, disaster relief, and public safety functions. NATO and Europe became increasingly engaged in security issues in Asia, participating in exercises in Asia and writing the first-ever NATO strategy regarding China. Nonetheless, Taiwan's own defense spending was far below the needed levels, jeopardizing prospects for winning more U.S. support.

Tsai was aware that skepticism remained about her role as commander in chief, and she dealt with this specific charge by visibly conducting defense policy as part of her daily business. She met frequently with the military leaders to communicate priorities in her "resolute defense, multi-domain deterrence" strategy to survive a frontal assault as well as the constant hybrid warfare being waged by China. Tsai routinely visited soldiers, bases, and exercises, with television cameras in tow.

She paid special attention to building up Taiwan's lagging capacity to address China's "cognitive warfare," which uses propaganda, disinformation, cyber, and other non-kinetic forms of attack. The legislature passed laws to counter foreign political interference and take down verified false material like deepfakes, which had increased by more than half in one year. Civil society groups created chatbot and fact-checking services to help users identify false information, and the government banned some Chinese social media platforms, formed rapid response teams to identify and debunk falsehoods, and launched information literacy classes in schools.

Tsai also launched a concerted diplomatic campaign to strengthen and expand Taiwan's relationships with countries around the world. She focused on quiet diplomacy with the United States and most of the rest of the world through trade and cultural offices. She also made use of Taiwan's membership in forty international organizations and observer status in others. Tsai prioritized bolstering relations with the United States, whose backing was essential to withstand an attack or blockade by China. She succeeded in greatly expanding U.S. political, military, and economic support during both the Trump and Biden administrations, as Washington's concerns about Xi's China grew.

In the face of Beijing's military buildup and frequent incursions into Taiwan's territorial waters, the United States became more vocal in warning China and supporting Taiwan. President Biden stated that the United States would come to Taiwan's defense in the event of a Chinese attack, taking a step away from the official U.S. policy of "strategic ambiguity." Taiwan began to have more regular contacts with U.S. officials at all levels. These high-profile contacts were met by increased saber-rattling from Beijing. When House Speaker Nancy Pelosi visited Taipei in 2022, China fired ballistic missiles over Taiwan and deployed hundreds of aircraft and naval vessels over and around Taiwan. The next year, when Tsai met with Speaker Kevin McCarthy in California in 2023, China again conducted encirclement exercises, flying hundreds of sorties into Taiwan's air defense zone, and deployed an aircraft carrier near its coastal waters. These became a new steady state as China tried to drive a wedge between Taiwan and the United States.

The third prong of Tsai's policy was an economic initiative called the New Southbound Policy, which sought to lessen Taiwan's heavy economic dependence on China by increasing trade with and investment in eighteen countries in the region, including Australia, Southeast Asia, and India. Taiwan offered its medical expertise to others, even as China blocked Taiwan's efforts to interact with the World Health Organization. The Southbound Policy yielded the most results in Australia and Southeast Asia, and in 2023, Taiwan concluded the first phase of a sweeping pact with the United States, the U.S.-Taiwan Initiative on 21st Century Trade, and the U.S. Congress ratified the accord. All these efforts produced a 70 percent increase in Taiwan's global exports.

STRENGTHENING TAIWAN'S DEMOCRACY

On the domestic policy front, Tsai bolstered Taiwan's resilience through continued social welfare programs, winning passage of pension, labor, and education reforms and a national childcare policy to help reduce the burden on working parents, especially mothers, who disproportionately shoulder unpaid care work. Tsai's government raised the hourly wage by 37 percent over her presidency. She also responded swiftly to the pandemic with border controls, quarantines, rigorous contact tracing, and mask wearing, with the result that Taiwan achieved a 94 percent vaccination rate with almost 90 percent receiving two shots. The government helped businesses adapt to hybrid and remote work with mass distribution of laptops. Despite the pandemic, Taiwan's economy achieved a 3 percent growth rate, exceeding China's for the first time.

Along with improving socioeconomic conditions for the entire population, Tsai pursued numerous measures to promote gender equality as a key part of strengthening democracy. In addition to legalizing same-sex marriage in 2019—the first country in Asia to do so—Tsai also asked Taiwan's legislature to strengthen its laws combatting harassment following a deluge of sexual harassment allegations as women gained the courage to name names in the global #MeToo movement. Gender discrimination laws were strengthened for the workplace and in schools, and in 2023, the OECD ranked Taiwan first in gender equality in Asia and sixth globally. Taiwan achieved one of the highest rates of women's political representation in the world. As of 2024, women comprised 42 percent of legislators, compared to 10 percent in Japan and 17 percent in South Korea. In meetings with youth, Tsai made efforts to encourage more young women to run for office.

Tsai's vision of strengthening Taiwan's democracy included recognition and support for victims of forty years of martial law and the many indigenous and early settler populations of Taiwan. She championed transitional justice measures for those jailed, tortured, and imprisoned under KMT martial law, including a law that provided restitution for victims from private and state assets seized by the KMT. Her efforts to elevate Taiwan's many indigenous populations began with an official apology for the injustices done to them, followed by a law to preserve their cultures and sixteen languages. Her government supported programs to recognize Taiwan's diverse culture, breaking with the traditional emphasis on Han Chinese culture. She attended indigenous ceremonies and took lessons to learn the Hakka language, as a woman descendant of Hakka, Minnan, and Paiwan forebears.

Tsai advanced the concept of "pluri-culturalism" as a way to overcome the old Chinese versus Taiwanese divide; the concept emphasized drawing from all cultures to form a new national identity rather than the multicultural concept of fostering separate identities.[10] Her government invested heavily in an array of projects to preserve Taiwan's cultural history in museums and celebrate it through live performances, multilingual television and radio stations, conferences, music, anime, virtual reality games, digital art, and a burgeoning fashion industry.

Gender equality remained a prominent feature of her presidency, from her awarding of the 2017 Presidential Cultural Award to LGBTQ rights pioneer Chi Chia-wei—the first government award bestowed on an LGBTQ person—to her last day as president, when she hosted a performance of an award-winning Taiwanese drag performer in the presidential offices.

TSAI'S LEGACY

Taiwan gained new visibility and confidence during Tsai's presidency, thanks to her steady hand in foreign and domestic policy even as China ratcheted up its pressure. As Tsai finished her second constitutionally limited term, voters elected her vice president as her successor in an endorsement of her formula of defending Taiwan without provoking intervention. In recognition of its robust democracy, the EIU Democracy Index ranked Taiwan the tenth-strongest democracy. Taiwan also remained firmly anchored in the global economy with its semiconductor industry powering the AI revolution.

After she left office, Tsai continued her leadership as an unofficial ambassador and global advocate for democracy, traveling frequently to counter Beijing's campaign of isolation and to rally democratic defenders to unite in a global network. In Canada, she accepted the John McCain Prize for Leadership in Public Service at the Halifax Security Forum. She called for greater support for Ukraine, noting that reining in Russia would also deter China. "Our collective response will make our democratic systems even stronger and more appealing," she said in her keynote speech. "We need to be more united than ever to ensure our security and protect our way of life." Speaking at the Copenhagen Democracy Summit in May 2025, she expressed alarm at the disruptive security and trade policy changes that the U.S. election had wrought. Urging leaders not to be "fickle" in their support of democracy, she held up Taiwan's model of resilience that "shows that democracy can survive and thrive even when under constant threat."

Tsai's governing record knocked down stereotypes about governance and leadership. She demonstrated that it was possible to pursue both a strong defense and progressive social policies, including expanding gender equality, without contradiction and with continuing popular support. While she suffered setbacks along the way, she achieved significant progress for the country in every realm of policy. Her tenure provided ample proof that a woman president can be equally or even more successful than a man in governing under extremely challenging circumstances. She will likely be considered one of the best leaders in Taiwan's history.

MAIA SANDU

DEFENDING MOLDOVA FROM RUSSIA'S HYBRID WARFARE

LIKE PRESIDENT TSAI, President Maia Sandu faced sexism and authoritarianism at home and abroad as she sought to strengthen democracy in Moldova. Sandu faced another of the world's leading authoritarian regimes, Russia, which sees the former Soviet republic of 2.9 million people not only as a wayward piece of territory that it has a right to reclaim but also as a strategic back door to Ukraine with its 1,200-kilometer border. Moscow has sought to weaken Moldova by cutting off energy and trade, waging disinformation and cyberattacks, and interfering in elections. Sandu's strategy to defend Moldova rested on joining the European Union, rooting out endemic corruption, and overcoming deep divisions in the country. Faced with persistent sexist attacks, Sandu won reelection in 2024 despite a massive vote-buying and disinformation campaign run from Moscow.

BUILDING A NEW DEMOCRACY

Born in 1972 in Rispeni, amid the fruit orchards and vineyards of the western corner of the Moldovan Soviet Socialist Republic, Maia Sandu graduated with a master's degree in international relations in 1991, two years after Moldova's independence. Like Tsai, she first entered government as a technocratic reformer, seeking to help build the country's democracy. She became frustrated with the lingering culture of corruption and decided to go to Harvard's school of government after the Communist Party was reelected in 2009 amid allegations of electoral fraud. "I witnessed the progress, but also the failures of the transition," she said of that period. "I always thought that the country could do better."[1] At the Kennedy School of Government, Sandu met people from around the world who had been trying for decades to improve their governments and realized that Moldova's road could be a long one. After graduation, she went to work for the World Bank's executive director in Washington.

When a new government was elected in Moldova in 2012, Sandu was offered the position of minister of education and accepted. "I decided to see whether I could do things that I was expecting from the ministers when I was a civil servant," she said. Returning home, however, she was confronted by sexist remarks and assertions that she was unqualified, despite her experience and credentials. "The resistance to change, the overwhelming problems in the education sector, the hate speech that I was confronted with, all made my life really difficult," she recalled.[2]

Sandu carried out numerous reforms as minister, the most famous of which was her campaign to end widespread cheating on the baccalaureate. The culture of corruption dating from the Soviet era included rampant cheating on tests. Parents paid for test results to ensure their children could enter university, and many educators tolerated or abetted the practice. Sandu had cameras installed in exam rooms and took other measures to prevent cheating. Pass rates dropped from 95 to 48 percent. The initial outcry from parents, students, and the public was enormous, she noted, "but then slowly they realized this was the only way to go."

As Sandu was trying to foster an ethical next generation, the country was hit by its worst corruption scandal, a massive bank heist that became known as the "theft of the century." Almost one billion dollars was stolen from three Moldovan banks in a complex scheme orchestrated by a rich businessman named Ilan Shor and his associates, who siphoned the money into offshore accounts. The government secretly bailed out the owners, to the tune of 12 percent of Moldova's GDP, and the country erupted in mass protest. Thousands of Moldovans poured into the streets in 2015 for a year of demonstrations that transformed into a civic movement calling for an end to corruption and ineffective government.

OVERCOMING SEXISM TO WIN THE PRESIDENCY

Sandu resigned from government and joined the protest movement. She founded the Party of Action and Solidarity and decided to run for president in 2016. "I never planned to become a minister, or prime minister, or president. I'm an introvert. I'm not somebody who likes to be in front of the people, to speak, to be in front of the cameras. But I had to learn," she said of her transition to politics. "Together with other people, we didn't want to live in a country which was run by corrupt politicians. We looked around and most of the political parties were led by corrupt people, which meant that we had two choices—either to leave the country, or to try to change politics."

Based on her reputation as a reformer, Sandu and her party gained popular support, but their campaign was a shoestring affair. She and her team lived on their savings, hiring only one staffer and renting just one office. Russia launched an intensive disinformation campaign that flooded Moldovan airwaves, press, social media, and streets. The country was divided between those who want to join the EU and those who sided with Russia. Anonymous leaflets plastered the country criticizing Sandu's support for joining the EU, alleging that she would "hand over a devastated country to the refugees, the homosexuals, and those who want to unite it with Romania."[3]

Sandu was also targeted with a stream of defamatory sexist attacks by leading figures who stoked the prejudices of a conservative religious society. In an extended televised diatribe, the Communist Party leader and former president Vladimir Voronin said a single woman with no children had no business running for president. "Everybody knows the rules of the presidential protocol: appearance in public must be together with spouse," he said.[4] He accused her of violating "family values" and called her "the laughingstock, the sin and the national disgrace of Moldova." The Russian Orthodox Church openly endorsed her rival, the Socialist Party leader Igor Dodon. A senior cleric attacked Sandu's fitness for office based on her single status, saying that "her attitude toward Christian morality . . . seems to diverge from normal principles."[5]

Sandu pushed back. "I have never thought being a single woman is a shame. Maybe it is a sin even to be a woman?" she retorted.[6] Rumors spread that her mother had been expelled from her church and that Sandu had sent her away to live in the United States. Sandu was deeply distressed at the attacks and lamented that so many people were willing to believe scurrilous gossip. She also rejected constant commentary about her face, hair, makeup, and dress, saying, "I did not participate in a beauty contest. I participated in the contest for the country." And to those who claimed that a single woman cannot lead a country, she said, "I want to remind them that everything we did at the Ministry of Education was for the children and for the good of the child."[7]

Despite the personal attacks, Sandu came in second but lost the runoff to her Russian-backed rival, Dodon. He had campaigned on closer ties with Moscow and joining its Eurasian union instead of the EU, and as president he frequently visited Russia.[8] Dodon's pitch resonated with many Moldovans who spoke Russian, watched Russian-language television, and attended the Russian Orthodox Church. About one-third of the country either sympathized with Russia or believed that it was fruitless to resist its influence. One of Moscow's prime levers was the breakaway region of Transnistria, where Russian-speaking separatists had declared their own state in 1990.

That sliver of territory along Moldova's border with Ukraine was the site of the electricity plant that powered much of Moldova, fueled by Russian gas. About 1,400 Russian troops remained after a brief armed conflict in 1990, marking the oldest of several "frozen conflicts" Russia created to stymie the former Soviet republics. Cowed by Russia's invasion and annexation of Crimea in 2014, many Moldovans clung to the idea that neutrality was their best defense.

Sandu did not give up. She ran in the 2019 parliamentary elections and her party came in second place. She made a tactical decision to form a government with Dodon to sideline the third-place contender, Vladimir Plahotniuc, the wealthiest and most powerful figure in the country who had been accused of playing a role in the bank scandal. Sandu thus briefly became Moldova's first woman prime minister. In her first acts, she called for international anti-corruption Magnitsky sanctions against him and the appointment of an independent prosecutor to root out Moldovan corruption. Both Plahotniuc and Ilan Shor, the architect of the heist, fled the country. The coalition government collapsed, however, when Dodon refused to back Sandu's anti-corruption proposals.[9]

DEFEATING HYBRID WARFARE AND STRENGTHENING DEMOCRACY

Sandu doggedly persisted, running for president in December 2020. She convinced the other reform parties to rally behind her candidacy to avoid splitting the vote and won a decisive victory with 58 percent. In her inaugural speech, Sandu appealed for unity in four languages, setting out a vision of progress and prosperity that EU membership could bring to everyone, including the Russian-speaking population in Transnistria as well as the pro-Russian Turkic population in the autonomous province of Gagauzia. When she first visited Gagauzia, Sandu had been shocked to see how neglected the province was. Most residents spoke only Russian, so she began a program to teach their native Gagauz language and Romanian. She launched education, infrastructure, and health projects with aid from Türkiye and promised Gagauzians that their unique history and culture would be preserved.

Sandu brought her own austere style to the presidency, presenting a stark contrast to the opulent lifestyles of Moldova's oligarchs and former leaders. She donated the presidency's expensive kitchen appliances to a vocational chef's school in Gagauzia, and on most days her mother brought her lunch to the presidential offices. She reduced the presidential motorcade and forbade it to block traffic. She opted not to live in the official residence and instead bought an apartment she shared with her sister.

Sandu called snap elections in 2021, seeking the parliamentary majority she needed to legislate a reform agenda. After five years of battling the pro-Russian parties and Russian interference, her party came in first with an outright majority of 52.8 percent in parliamentary elections. Amid disruption caused by the global pandemic, she launched her program with a team of fellow reformers, including Natalia Gavrilița, a fellow Kennedy School graduate and finance minister in her first cabinet, who served as prime minister from 2021 to 2023. Cristina Gherasimov became her foreign policy adviser, chief of staff, and later minister for EU integration. Mihail Popșoi, a political scientist and vice president of her party, became foreign minister.

Russia's invasion of Ukraine on February 24, 2022 triggered a crisis in next-door Moldova as more than a million Ukrainians arrived. Moldovans opened their doors to feed and house the refugees, more than one hundred thousand of whom remained while others moved elsewhere in Europe. In retaliation for Moldova's vocal support for Ukraine and the closing of its airspace to Russia, Moscow cut gas and trade. Soon after, Ukraine was forced to stop sending electricity to Moldova as Russian bombardments crippled its energy infrastructure. Amid food and fertilizer shortages, inflation rose to 35 percent.

Sandu formulated a strategy, the centerpiece of which was for Moldova to gain rapid accession to the European Union. The EU soon accepted the country's application and provided more than two billion euros in the coming years, enabling Moldova to heat homes, develop new energy and trade partners, and enact governance reforms to meet EU standards. The EU and NATO provided security training and supplied a short-range missile defense system to ward off the drones and missiles that occasionally landed in its territory. EU teams bolstered Moldova's ability to identify and counter disinformation, cyberattacks, bomb threats, and hoaxes. The United States also responded with an early visit from U.S. Secretary of State Tony Blinken and $755 million in assistance over the coming three years.

Sandu launched a wider diplomatic campaign to gain visibility and support for Moldova, seeking to establish the country as a reliable partner and bulwark against Russian encroachment. She found a strong ally in French President Emmanuel Macron, who founded the European Political Community (EPC) in 2022 as a forum to include European countries outside the EU fold. Sandu proposed that she host the second EPC summit, and in 2023, forty-five heads of state and EU leaders flew into Chisinau, a remarkable show of support for the tiny country in the shadow of Russia's war. Sandu continued to travel abroad to meet her counterparts and speak at global gatherings; at the third EPC summit, she and Macron spoke about the defense of democracy, and at the EU's European People's Party congress, she emphasized her country's defiant stand against Russian aggression. "Today, Moldova is not ON the table, as Russia desired; instead, Moldova is AT the table," she said. "Our people have made a sovereign and conscious choice not to be forcefully consigned to Russia's sphere of influence again."[10]

Sandu's campaign achieved a critical breakthrough in October 2022, when the U.S. Treasury Department announced sweeping sanctions on Shor, Plahotniuc, and a host of Moldovan and Russian individuals, organizations, and companies for actions that "expose not only Russia's covert strategy in Moldova, but also demonstrate how corruption undermines the rule of law."[11] The United States named Shor, his political party, his Russian pop star wife, Russian intelligence agents, businessmen, and companies as part of an ongoing enterprise to destabilize Sandu's government, impede Moldova's EU bid, and return Moldova to Russia's sphere of influence. The department cited Plahotniuc for "capturing and corrupting Moldova's state institutions" via a wide range of acts including weaponizing law enforcement, courts, media, and the electoral apparatus against rivals, as well as bribery, coercion, and theft of state funds and private assets.

This public affirmation of the depth of Moldovan corruption and the central role of Russia gained further traction as the UK and EU added their own sanctions. The supporting evidence and sanctions blacklisted key individuals and froze funds, aiding Moldova's pursuit of legal remedy and legislative reform. Moldovan courts sentenced Shor in absentia and ordered the confiscation of $290 million of his assets.[12] Moldova also initiated a vetting process for judges and culled one-third of the bench for not meeting standards or providing documentation that their assets were obtained legitimately. Moldova adopted procedural reforms recommended by the Council of Europe; by 2024, it had implemented thirteen of eighteen corruption prevention measures for parliament, judges, and prosecutors and had initiated four others.[13]

In a bid to halt Moldova's progress and restore the dominance of its pro-Russian political parties, Russia dramatically escalated its hybrid campaign against Sandu and her government. In 2023, Ukrainian intelligence uncovered a large-scale effort by Russia, through its paramilitary Wagner Group, to train violent agitators to unseat Sandu. She revealed the coup plot in a press conference, and Washington verified the details in subsequent statements.[14] She also ejected forty-five of the seventy officials posted to Russia's Chisinau embassy, a building with a forest of antennas bristling from its rooftop.[15]

As the 2024 presidential election campaign got under way, Russia spent millions of dollars to defeat Sandu in a complex scheme managed and paid for by Russian intelligence, with Shor, who had moved to Russia, as the front man. As the head of the Victory Bloc, he bought hundreds of ads attacking Sandu under his own name on Facebook, despite a company policy banning convicted felons from conducting such activity.[16] Telegram was used to recruit and pay Moldovans to organize and attend protests, enlist others, and buy votes. A Russian-based network ferried in cash. Moldovans were also paid from Russian bank accounts they could access through QR codes. Shor recruited and funded an unknown candidate, Evgenia Gutsul, to win the governorship of Gagauzia. She then became another conduit for dispersing Russian funds.[17]

Sandu faced a crowded field of ten candidates, many of them recruited by Shor and Russia to draw votes away from her. Sandu decided to call a simultaneous referendum on joining the EU to enshrine the support in the constitution so that even if she lost, the path to EU membership would be secure. Polls showed that a comfortable majority favored joining the EU, but given the electoral interference effort under way, it was a gamble. Sandu asked voters to pass the referendum, with the argument that "joining the European Union is Moldova's Marshall Plan."

The European Union announced the approval of Moldova's application for membership and formally opened the accession process, and U.S. and EU officials paid visits to Chisinau to show their support. On election night, October 24, 2024, supporters in Sandu's campaign headquarters anxiously watched as returns came in. Sandu was forced into a runoff with 42 percent of the vote. Even more concerning was the razor-thin 50.4 percent vote in favor of EU membership, with the winning margin provided by diaspora voters. The team was shocked at the narrow margin since polls had shown support for joining the EU as high as 70 percent.

In later days, the level of interference was documented; Moldova's security service reported that more than 130,000 votes had been bought.[18] A nonprofit research organization reported that 90 percent of the online gendered disinformation in Moldova was directed at Sandu; the online campaign relied heavily on bots, fake accounts, and troll farms as well as deepfake videos that were viewed millions of times.[19] The deepfakes included Sandu in a hijab, telling voters she was resigning and urging them to vote for a Shor-backed party, and clips of Hollywood stars saying "let's bring down Sandu."

WEIGHING MOLDOVA'S PROGRESS AND SANDU'S LEADERSHIP

Sandu won the November 2024 runoff with 55 percent of the vote, despite what the EU called "unprecedented interference [that] sought to undermine the country's democratic institutions and its EU path."[20] In a year in which more than half the world's population went to the polls, Moldova was one of the few democracies that reelected an incumbent leader. Moldova had also made steady progress in closing its gender gap, reaching eighth place in the World Economic Forum's ranking with women leaders across government, including 40 percent of cabinet members and in parliament. Moldova's parliament had also passed measures to reduce disinformation and sexism in advertising, social media, and media.

Moldova had achieved successes in fending off Russia's hybrid warfare. Moldova's nascent Cyber Security Agency defended critical infrastructure and government agencies from hacks and denial of service attacks, and a Strategic Communications Center identified narratives and countered their propagation.[21] To prevail against internationally networked threats required ongoing support from tech companies and other governments, as well as expensive cybersecurity software like Cloudflare.

Moldova had made remarkable progress in energy security, shifting from Russia to European and U.S. markets for gas. It pioneered the use of Greece's pipeline to bring gas north and rechanneled routes to underground storage tanks. According to energy minister Dorin Junghietu, Moldova had increased its renewable energy production eightfold, and high-voltage lines would begin supplying most of the country's electricity from Romania at the end of 2025.[22] Moldova's economy was largely weaned from Russia, even as the country still struggled with inflation and wartime conditions. The great majority of its trade, investment, and travel had shifted to Europe, spurring new markets for its wine and fruit; even Transnistrians were getting Moldovan passports and trading with Europe.

Moldovans had become increasingly aware of the degree to which manipulation and disinformation were affecting their country. In a survey, two-thirds of Moldovans said they saw foreign manipulation as a serious problem, and 54 percent believed social media platforms were increasing division in the country.[23] Moreover, a greater number of people were beginning to do something about it. *Ziarul de Garda*, an investigative newspaper founded by two women in 2004, became the country's largest paper in 2024 thanks to its exposure of the Telegram network to buy votes and pay agitators to campaign against Sandu. Alina Radu, the paper's cofounder and executive editor, said that readers sent in tips and helped the investigative reporters who went undercover to film and record the operation in action. She called it a milestone for a country where the largest paper had been Russian owned.[24]

Progress on judicial reform was slow, however. Sandu acknowledged that voters were disappointed that more progress had not been made in reforming the justice system to bring perpetrators to account. "I myself thought that we would be able to reform justice sooner, but unfortunately, we did not find enough support within the system," she said. Radu agreed with the assessment, saying that "the justice reform has not . . . reached the point that would make the path of reform irreversible." She cited the depth of the corruption and the fact the courts, which must rule on the expulsion of judges, tended to protect corrupt individuals.

Sandu sought to address frustrations in frequent visits to the countryside, explaining that she could not directly remove judges or prosecutors or bring back stolen assets and criminals from foreign countries. She underlined the important of face-to-face conversations. "If you don't visit, people believe that you are disconnected, that you don't know about their problems." Visiting Costesti in May 2025, she walked in the town parade, gave a speech, and spent an hour talking to townspeople and taking dozens of selfies with women and girls dressed in national costumes. She drove next in her two-car caravan to the village of Lozova to speak to the crowd in a pouring rain and, despite being drenched, stayed on to chat with villagers. She sought to fulfill the pledge she had made on election night to be a "president for all. I have heard your voice—both from those who support me and those who voted differently. No matter your voting choice, we all want to live in peace, in harmony, and to have a better life. I assure you that this is my primary goal for the coming years."[25]

About one-third of Moldovans regularly rated Sandu as the country's most trusted public figure, 10 percent ahead of any other figures, and many expatriates had returned to help her, inspired by her probity and determination. Despite success in reforms and external support, the war in Ukraine imposed a heavy economic cost, with many pensioners struggling to make ends meet. Assessing her experience, Sandu noted that she had faced hurdles as a woman leader but had also received support. When she faced sexist attacks, many organizations came to her defense, unlike the many less visible women candidates for mayor who did not receive that attention. While quotas in Moldova's parliament had helped raise women's visibility, physical violence against women was still a severe problem in the country. Sandu was proud that her election had disproven those who believed Moldova was not ready for a woman president. She said that voters chose "someone they thought was honest and . . . prepared to run the country." Another advantage was her objective of securing peace. "There are more [voters] who trust that I'll preserve peace than my opponent. Many would say a woman . . . will do her best to use diplomatic measures and tools to make sure that we have peace."

Sandu hoped to achieve EU membership by the end of her presidential term in December 2029. The Russian-backed campaign again ramped up in 2025 to defeat her party in parliamentary elections by means of vote-buying, armed agitators, and disinformation that accused Sandu of trafficking Ukrainian refugee children and buying Brad Pitt's sperm. European leaders visited and the EU imposed sanctions on figures connected to the interference, but the previous U.S. assistance for election integrity, cybersecurity, and independent journalism had been cut. In a long-sought breakthrough, the oligarch Plahotniuc was extradited to Moldova to stand trial for the bank theft Moldovans called the "heist of the century" just days before the election. The country gave Sandu's party a majority in the parliamentary elections, proving that a small country could indeed stand up to Russia and chart its own course.

Sandu's successes were powered by a new Moldovan generation that wanted to break free of Russian influence and corruption, but her leadership became a symbol of fortitude as the country faced severe outside pressure and internal division. She overcame sexism, formed her own party, and won successive elections that endorsed her strategy of reforms and accession to EU membership to consolidate democracy and protect

Moldova from continued Russian hybrid warfare. The obstacles arrayed against this project were substantial: the war in Ukraine, Russian influence and interference, economic difficulties, and increased migration of young Moldovans. The journey was not finished, but Sandu had achieved reforms, energy and economic resilience, and a constitutional commitment to EU membership. Despite the conservative society, she also advanced gender equality laws and, through her leadership, broke down the masculine stereotype of the top offices of prime minister and president. While progress depended crucially on Europe's continued support for both Moldova and Ukraine, her tenure set a foundation for the country to break free of corruption and Russian influences and continue its democratic development.

Chapter Seven

KAJA KALLAS

STIFFENING EUROPE'S DEFENSES AGAINST RUSSIA

AS ESTONIA'S FIRST FEMALE PRIME MINISTER from 2021 to 2024, Kaja Kallas became known for her leadership in opposing Russia's invasion of Ukraine and hybrid warfare against Europe. Her government sent early aid and training to Ukraine; she was the first to authorize using frozen Russian assets for Ukraine's defense and to propose holding Putin accountable for war crimes.[1] At home, Kallas strengthened defenses and economic resilience while also expanding gender equality as the second country in Eastern Europe to legalize same-sex marriage. Her achievements led her to a wider leadership role in Europe as an EU vice president and high representative for foreign affairs and security in late 2024.

KALLAS'S PATH TO POLITICS AND ENCOUNTERS WITH SEXISM

Estonia was the first Soviet republic to break away from the Soviet Union and achieved formal independence in 1991. The relatively young country opened opportunities for women to participate in building democracy, and a political crisis led Kallas into politics. Her father and great grandfather had played prominent roles in Estonia's resistance and liberation, but she sought to blaze her own path. She opted for a law career to help build the burgeoning free market economy and made partner at age twenty-seven, the first woman in her firm to do so. When she found out that her partnership agreement gave her a much smaller share in return for bringing in a much larger share of the work, she asked for equal treatment. "If my money that I bring to the firm is somehow of less quality than the money the boys are bringing in, I'm leaving the firm," she told the senior partner.[2] He did not accede, so she quit. Her male colleagues were shocked and told her they would have fought on her behalf; she took it as an early lesson to always seek allies. "Never fight alone. You have allies." She went to a new firm, built her business, and made partner again. But at age thirty-three, Kallas was ready for a new challenge.

She was encouraged by friends to go into politics after writing some articles and giving speeches about reforming Estonia's laws to increase its competitiveness. She was still reluctant to be compared to her father for fear she would not measure up, but eventually relented. "I guess it's in my blood," she said. She joined the Reform Party, which her father had founded, and was elected to parliament in 2011. She came in ready to make changes: Many leaders had been involved in corruption scandals, and she proposed that parliament adopt a code of conduct to require greater transparency in funding. Many legislators, including members of her own party were reluctant to support a proposal that would subject them to greater scrutiny, but in the end, she won passage of the law.

Being the daughter of a former prime minister did not protect Kallas from sexism and may have exacerbated sexist suggestions that her ideas came from her father. During her two terms in parliament, including as chair of the economic commission, she was subjected to frequent bullying. She was ridiculed for being polite, having nothing to say, being too pretty, and being unqualified, although her qualifications exceeded those of many legislators. Tired of the hostile environment, Kallas decided to run for a seat in the European Parliament, which she won, and decamped to Brussels in 2014.

Divorced from her husband, Kallas made her own way as a single mother with a young son. She found the climate of the European Parliament much friendlier than the one she had left behind in Tallinn. Many members knew of Estonia's role as a leading digital innovator and wanted to learn from its experience. She rapidly collected assignments and dove into the work. In Brussels she felt appreciated for her substance, in contrast to Tallinn, where her family ties, gender, and appearance were often the focus of attention. Also, more women served in the European Parliament, including in leadership positions, and gender equality was woven into EU guidelines.

Kallas's four years in the European Parliament gave her a deep appreciation of Europe's diversity as a continent of many small countries. The arts of negotiation and compromise, which she had learned in her legal career, were essential to forge agreements among the twenty-seven member states of the European Union. Kallas also realized the vast chasm of experience and perception between Western and Eastern Europe; those who had experienced occupation by the Soviet Union had very different experiences that colored their views of Russia.

Kallas's personal history regarding Russia ran deep. Her grandmother and mother, then a six-month old baby, were deported from Estonia to Siberia in Operation Priboi in 1949, in a truck, her grandmother taking her sewing machine to provide for them as a seamstress. In all, more than ninety thousand Estonians were interned in Siberian prison camps. Kallas, who was fourteen when Estonia regained its freedom in 1991, shared Eastern Europe's alarm as Russia reacted to the color revolutions of the 2000s with sabotage, disinformation, and other coercive tactics.[3] They were acutely aware that history could be reversed. "We were forgotten for fifty years behind the Iron Curtain, and we never want to experience that again," she said.

In Brussels, Kallas took a leading role in responding to Russia's 2014 stealth invasion of Ukraine and its annexation of Crimea. She became vice chair of the parliament's EU-Ukraine Cooperation Commission, which prepared proposals and gathered support for financial aid packages, trade concessions, and technical advice on the justice, legal, and economic reforms that Ukraine would need to implement to be accepted for membership in the EU. She sought to integrate Europe's energy and digital markets and lower trade barriers to increase its resilience. For her work on Ukraine, creating Europe's Single Digital Market, instituting e-privacy reforms, strengthening EU competitiveness, and reducing trade barriers, *Politico* magazine named her one of forty top legislators in Brussels in 2019.

CALLED TO LEAD AMID CRISIS, KALLAS FORMS A GOVERNMENT OF GENDER PARITY

The leader of Estonia's Reform Party, which was riven by internal divisions and falling in the polls, texted Kallas to say that he was resigning and had just told the press that he thought she should become the next party leader. She was stunned that he would make such a statement without first consulting her. Press calls started pouring in, and Kallas was once again reminded of the irritations she had faced in Tallinn. She had not intended to move back to Estonia at that time, but she relented. "The party saw me as the unifier," she said, and she left Brussels before the end of her term. Back in Tallinn, she worked to patch up the party's divisions and public image before leading it to elections in 2019.

Kallas's party came in first, besting the governing Centre Party, which came in second. But in talks to form a coalition, the Centre leader rejected the terms Kallas proposed and instead formed a three-party coalition including the far-right

EKRE party, founded in 2015. It was the first time that the far right formed part of an Estonian government, and the populist anti-EU, anti-immigrant, antigay, anti-U.S. party proved to be predictably disruptive. The coalition government collapsed in a year amid a wave of scandals and resignations. President Kersti Kaljulaid, Estonia's first woman in the role, then turned to Kallas to form a government. She succeeded in doing so, and in January 2021, at age forty-three, became the first woman to serve as prime minister of Estonia. Kallas's cabinet was the first in Estonia's history to include women in half of the ministerial positions, which she had made a condition of her offer to potential coalition partners.

Kallas faced severe domestic economic problems caused by the COVID-19 pandemic, including a fiscal crisis caused by the slowing economy, inflation, and the previous government's deficit spending. The EU guidelines capped governments' deficit spending at 3 percent, so she pushed through unpopular budget cuts while seeking to maintain essential services. She acknowledged the difficult times the country was going through and sought to cushion the blow for the poorest Estonians without violating the EU spending rules.

Returning to the pink parliament building perched on a hill above Tallinn's medieval old city, Kallas thought she was prepared for the jousting environment, but now that she was in charge, she faced an even greater onslaught of sexism and heckling. After she was elected to lead her party, friends suggested that she alter her profile to blunt the sexist attacks. They counseled her to cut her hair, wear suits, and lower her voice. Some even suggested she wear glasses and gain weight.

Kallas had no intention of changing herself—a concession to sexism that she would not make. She did not want to fit in with the boys or appear more manlike, insisting that women should present themselves however they wish. She said, "I prefer dresses, and I will continue to dress the way I like."[4]

She found the EKRE party's abuse particularly crude. Its slash-and-burn politics had gained a quarter of the population's support, as part of the global trend of rising right-wing populism. Its legislators hurled sexist insults at her during hours-long parliamentary debates. They accused her of being mentally ill and challenged her fitness for office, saying things like "Tell me, flower, how did you end up here?"[5] Kallas maintained her composure in these ordeals and calmly requested that debates be conducted around substantive critiques and policy. As a lawyer, Kallas relished a good debate but was deeply bothered by the ubiquity of sexist and demeaning treatment in the Estonian press and politics. When she was first elected to Estonia's parliament, she had been criticized for being overly deferential and polite; after she adopted a tougher tone, she was called annoying and difficult. Double standards cropped up no matter what she did. When she closed an event by saying that she had to get home to her family, a colleague urged her to simply say she had another meeting; when she did that, people asked who was taking care of the family. "Nobody asks the man who cooks the dinner or takes care of the children," she remarked.

Kallas continued to ponder what could be done about sexism and uncivil behavior. She found tips for dealing with bullies in a book by a Stanford professor, *The Asshole Guide to*

Survival: How to Deal with People Who Treat You Like Dirt. She was not content with merely enduring the phenomenon; she wanted to change it. She talked more openly about the issue than many women leaders, sharing her experience, encouraging women to assert themselves in leadership roles, and discussing the effects of abusive public discourse on democracy.

DEFENDING AND STRENGTHENING DEMOCRACY IN THE FACE OF RUSSIAN AGGRESSION

In the spring of 2021, Kallas was immediately alarmed by the news of Russia massing troops on Ukraine's border and moving missiles into Crimea. At a meeting of the European Council, as a new prime minister at the table, she surprised her counterparts by speaking out against German Chancellor Merkel's proposal to hold talks with Putin. She warned that Putin was likely to make demands and seek concessions without giving anything in return. It would be better, she suggested, to close loopholes in the leaky sanctions imposed on Russia after its annexation of Crimea in 2014.

Kallas's alarm increased when Putin sent two draft agreements to Washington and Brussels in December that revealed his larger objective. The documents called for NATO to pull back troop deployments to its 1997 borders, which would effectively cast Eastern and Central Europe outside the alliance's protective umbrella and subject them to the same coercion and domination that Putin was applying to countries on Russia's periphery. Kallas saw the proposals as a barely veiled threat: Unless NATO willingly drew back from Russia's borders, Russia would unilaterally expand its periphery by invading Ukraine. When Russia invaded Ukraine two months later, Kallas immediately spoke out. "Russia's widespread aggression is a threat to the entire world and to all NATO countries," she said in the first of dozens of speeches. "The most effective response to Russia's aggression is unity." From that moment, Kallas moved to the forefront of European action, making proposals, taking initiatives at home, and using them to prod Western Europe to send commensurate military, humanitarian, and economic assistance.

Estonia immediately sent its own stockpiles of howitzers, Javelin and Milan anti-tank missiles, arms, and munitions to Kyiv, along with military advisers. It boosted its own defense budget—already one of the highest in NATO at 3 percent of GDP—and pledged ongoing military aid to Ukraine amounting to 1 percent of its GDP. Kallas urged the rest of Europe to make concrete pledges. She became one of the Ukrainian president's most visible supporters, welcoming him to Tallinn and visiting him in Kyiv. Echoing his mantra, she said, "Freedom must be armed better than tyranny. That's our common motto. That's why the number one focus are arms, ammunition, and training—they all must continue at a scale sufficient for Ukraine to win the war."[6] Estonia spent five hundred million euros, 1.66 percent of its GDP, to provide weapons, field hospitals, communication and medical equipment, humanitarian and reconstruction aid, and sanctuary for more than 54,000 Ukrainian refugees. Estonia was one of the first countries to sign a ten-year defense pact guaranteeing Ukraine a minimum of 0.25 percent of its GDP in annual assistance.[7]

Estonians overwhelmingly supported Kallas's actions. Resistance was part of their history. Estonians had waged long-term guerrilla war against Russian forces, and it retained a volunteer force, the Estonian Defense League, which swelled to thirty thousand after Russia's invasion of Ukraine. For years the government had rehearsed and prepared for a "whole of society" mobilization with regularly updated strategies, stockpiles, interagency plans and councils, and annual callups and exercises. Estonia's defensive action predated the Russian invasion of Ukraine. Russia had been probing Estonia for years in a constant campaign of destabilization and propaganda designed to intimidate Estonians and sow resentment among the country's substantial Russian-speaking population, which lives primarily along the eastern border. Russian agents surveilled the watery border near Narva with spies on skiffs posing as fishermen, and Estonian police and border guards were frequently harassed or spirited into Russia.

Estonia had felt it was already at war with Russia, although Western publics had been slow to recognize it. Russia had launched the first mass cyberattack against another country in 2007. The denial-of-service attack crippled Estonia's government, banks, and media for days. The attack awakened NATO militaries to the need to update their understanding of Russian warfare. Russia has adapted the old Soviet Union playbook of "active measures" to a new form of all-domain hybrid warfare to weaken and subvert the West. NATO set up a Cyber Defense Center in the country, and Estonia's intelligence service published detailed annual reports of Russian subversion. NATO also deployed defensive battalions to the Baltic states, which were considered the likeliest route should Russia invade Europe. Russia would use an armed enclave, Kaliningrad, on the Baltic Sea, where it stationed a naval fleet. In conjunction with its Ukrainian invasion, Russia moved Iskander missiles to Kaliningrad, began aggressive aerial patrols in the Baltic Sea, and even jammed communications of civilian flights.

In response, Kallas raised defense spending to 3.4 percent of GDP and moved to shore up Estonia's economy against further pressure and retaliation from Russia. The Baltics had been working to achieve energy independence from Russia and cut off its gas purchases in 2022. Kallas set a target for totally renewable electricity by 2030 and achieved 65 percent by 2023.

While most Estonians backed the Kallas government's actions, she faced opposition from the more neutral Centre in her coalition. She dismissed the Centre party to govern as a minority government, stating that she had hoped the Russian invasion would have "opened the eyes of all parties . . . to how important it is for Estonia's independence to have a unified understanding of the dangers we face as a country neighboring Russia." She noted that only two Centre ministers held NATO security clearances, which complicated deliberations within the cabinet. The opposition EKRE also kept up its outlier position against aid and admitting Ukrainian refugees, arguing that the government was provoking tensions with Russia.

Kallas prevailed over these views in March 2023 general elections when voters gave her Reform Party a wider margin.

She formed a coalition government with the new Estonia 200 party and the Social Democrats. On June 23, 2023, a clear summer day at the height of the strawberry harvest in central Estonia, she laid a wreath honoring Estonians who had fought for their country's liberation in 1919. The sunny central plaza in Viljandi was packed with families and members of the Estonian Defense League, young and old volunteers who trained to deliver humanitarian relief and first aid as part of the whole-of-country defense strategy. Thanking the volunteers and soldiers in their multicolored regalia, Kallas noted that bombs were dropping on Ukraine just 1,300 kilometers away. "The people of Estonia know that freedom is not self-evident," she said. "Freedom must be fought for, and it is worth fighting for."[8] She praised the high level of readiness of Estonia's forces. An Estonian woman leaning on the barricade surrounding the plaza said, "She's our Galadriel," referring to J.R.R. Tolkien's elfin warrior queen.

ASSERTING A LEADERSHIP ROLE IN EUROPE

Kallas used Estonia's example to push Europe to do more for Ukraine, put more pressure on Russia, and shore up its own languishing defense capacity. She proposed that Europe commit to producing one million artillery shells and use frozen Russian assets, which were mostly held in Europe, to fund Ukraine's defense and rebuild its destroyed infrastructure. She led the way by passing the first law legalizing use of the frozen assets and adopting a Ukrainian province as the focus of its reconstruction aid. She urged Europe to tighten and extend sanctions on Russian trade that continued to fund the country's war machine. As Ukrainian casualties mounted into the tens of thousands and its manpower shortages became acute, Kallas urged fellow NATO members to send more air defenses, jets, and tanks and to allow Ukraine to use that weaponry to strike the Russian bases launching air and missile attacks. She advocated fast-tracking Ukraine's admission to NATO as well as its rapid accession to the EU. Kallas also made the case for charging Putin with the crime of aggression, which would require the convening of an international tribunal, as essential to deter any further aggression. Without accountability, she argued at the Munich Security Conference, Russia would not learn the lesson that Nazi Germany had learned.[9]

Kallas believed the West was providing too little, too late. As Russia launched its counteroffensive in December 2023, she urged: "If there is anything else Europe can do or provide, it must be done right now and immediately. I want to believe that we will be able to agree during this week's European Council on sanctions, the use of frozen assets, economic and military assistance, and on inviting Ukraine to accession negotiations, and thereby encourage all the other countries in the world. Putin must understand that time is against him, not in his favor."[10]

She argued against those who thought Ukraine should negotiate a settlement, on the grounds that it would leave Russian troops in Ukraine and compromise its sovereignty. "The only path to peace is to push Russia out of Ukraine," she wrote in *Foreign Affairs*.[11] She urged other countries not to be cowed by fears that Putin would escalate with attacks into Europe or resort to tactical nuclear weapons. "The definition of terrorism is to make us afraid so that we will refrain from the decisions that we would otherwise make," she said.[12] For her strong stand, Kallas was frequently called Europe's new Iron Lady. Some Western Europeans viewed her as too hawkish, yet as Russia's punishing attacks and grisly atrocities mounted, her predictions about Putin and Ukraine's ability to resist proved accurate, and many of her proposals were embraced.

Kallas put herself forward as a candidate for NATO secretary-general in a characteristically bold move. She argued that the Baltic states had earned the right to leadership positions in NATO and the EU; they had made outsize contributions since joining both organizations, proving they were not just small states that had to be protected. Estonia spent 3 percent of GDP on defense at a time when only six NATO members had met the 2 percent threshold agreed upon years earlier. A NATO secretary-general from Estonia would send a clear message to Russia that the West would not bow to Putin's ongoing threats and predation. In the end, however, the Biden administration backed Dutch Prime Minister Mark Rutte.

EXPANDING DEMOCRACY THROUGH GENDER RIGHTS AND INCLUSION

At home, Kallas pushed through gender equality initiatives as well as other social reforms, despite the difficult economic climate. Her electoral victory in March 2023 enabled her to pass legalization of same-sex marriage over conservative parties' objections, making Estonia the second country in Eastern Europe to do so. She strengthened the existing gender equality act and pushed for closing the gender pay gap, increasing pay transparency, and training more women in technology fields. Kallas achieved gender balance in all three of her cabinets and spoke frequently about the need for more reforms. Touting Estonia's flexible parental leave and the need to share childcare work at the 2023 Democracy Summit, she said, "Gender equality is not only a matter of justice but also a matter of economic growth and competitiveness."

Kallas hoped to encourage more women to pursue political careers and proposed anti–hate speech measures to make their path easier than hers had been. She gave women leadership roles and encouraged others to run for parliament to increase their share from the 2024 level of 28.7 percent. As a role model, she hoped her habit of speaking out would encourage women to ask for what they deserve and avoid underestimating their abilities. Always ready to recommend books, she praised the memoir of Katherine Graham, publisher and editor of the *Washington Post*, for its frank description of her initial diffidence and the challenges of becoming a powerful leader in a city overwhelmingly dominated by men. Kallas faced harsh criticism in the summer of 2023 when it became known that her husband was a shareholder in a company doing business in Russia, in contradiction to Kallas's policy of ending economic ties with Russia. The security services had vetted the couple's finances and business dealings, but the press and political rivals called for her resignation. The Reform Party reelected her as its leader by a two-thirds vote.

Kallas sought to play an expanded role in Europe, and in 2024 she was elected vice president of the European Commission as well as the European Union's High Representative for Foreign Affairs and Security Policy. Joining the leadership team of Commission president Ursula von der Leyen, Kallas brought additional influence as a former head of government. She immediately leaned forward to respond to the new Trump administration's policy of cutting aid to Ukraine and putting pressure on it to cede to Putin's demands. Kallas warned that "isolationism has never worked well for America."[13] Together with von der Leyen, Kallas continued to rally the EU to provide more aid and beef up integrated European defense industries. She also prioritized EU peace building in the Middle East and EU diplomacy to address conflict in the Western Balkans.

Kallas's rise to leadership was aided by the opportunities created in a post-Soviet democracy and a crisis in her political party. She persevered against persistent sexism as she became Estonia's first woman prime minister, won reelection, and ascended to a leadership role in Europe. Her strong stand on defense helped break down the masculine stereotype of leadership, and her willingness to put herself forward for higher office stood as encouragement to future women leaders. She forthrightly challenged sexist behavior and sought legislative and cultural remedies to the problem as hampering democracy. She used her leadership to expand legal protections for women and advance gender equality, again proving that there is no contradiction between a strong national security policy and inclusive social policies.

Chapter Eight

VJOSA OSMANI-SADRIU

BUILDING DEMOCRACY IN SERBIA'S SHADOW

VJOSA OSMANI-SADRIU became the second women to serve as president of Kosovo, Europe's newest country, in 2020. Kosovo emerged from the 1999 NATO intervention to stop Serbia's war of ethnic cleansing. Its situation remained precarious because of continued destabilization by Serbia, which refused to recognize the country, and internal conflict with the Serbian minority, which was stoked by Belgrade. As president in Kosovo's dual executive system, Osmani held fewer powers than her coalition partner, Prime Minister Albin Kurti, but because of her experience and stature, she exercised considerable influence. From an early age, Osmani was involved in the creation of Kosovo as an activist, lawyer, and legislator. She helped write its constitution and defend its declaration of independence, and as a legislator, she fought for the rule of law and women's rights. Her formal powers as president included serving as commander in chief and leading international relations, both of which were important as Kosovo sought to expand its defenses, gain wider international recognition, and attain membership in international bodies. With Russian backing, Serbia continued to block Kosovo's membership in the United Nations, but Osmani expanded the number of countries that formally recognized the country and fostered crucial ties with the United States and NATO, which maintained a peacekeeping force in northern Serbia.

BUILDING KOSOVO'S DEMOCRACY

As a young woman, Vjosa Osmani was drawn into politics as she listened to her father and his friends discuss Kosovo's liberation struggle in the family living room. She joined the Democratic League of Kosovo (LDK), the party of Ibrahim Rugova, who led the country's nonviolent movement for independence. She stayed the course even after a Serbian soldier invaded their house and shoved the barrel of his AK-47 into her mouth during the ethnic cleansing campaign in which Serbian forces killed and displaced tens of thousands of ethnic Albanians and raped thousands of women. At the United States' behest, NATO intervened to end the fighting in 1999. The country lay in ruins, as Kosovars began to build a democracy.

"Everything had to be built from scratch," Osmani recalled. "It was like we were emerging from the ashes, and there was a sense that everyone had to do something."[1] Osmani earned a master's and a doctorate in law at the University of Pittsburgh, with a dissertation on UN law and the status of Kosovo. Her former professor, Fatmir Sejdiu, became president of the aspiring republic in 2006 and invited her to join his team. She served as his chief of staff, senior legal adviser, and representative on the commission that drafted Kosovo's constitution. Kosovo declared independence in 2008, and when Serbia disputed the move, Osmani helped win the case before the International Court of Justice.

Osmani ran for parliament in 2010, winning the support of young Kosovars for her anti-corruption stand, which helped her surmount sexism in the heavily male-dominated political parties. A rising star, Osmani increasingly clashed with her LDK party leader Isa Mustafa over his decision to form a coalition government with the rival PDK party and to support the election of its leader Ibrahim Thaci as president in 2016. In 2019, recognizing that Osmani was the party's most popular politician, the LDK chose her to lead its party list in the elections. She narrowly lost to the Self-Determination (Vetëvendosje) party of Albin Kurti.[2]

The rise of Osmani and Kurti marked a generational shift in Kosovo politics, as voters tired of the old-guard leaders who had failed to bring peace or prosperity after twenty years. Osmani became the first women elected as speaker of parliament, but a tumultuous year followed as she continued to battle her party leadership, which toppled Kurti's government with a no-confidence vote. She became acting president when Kosovo's sitting President Thaci resigned to face war crime charges brought by the Kosovo Special Tribunal. Osmani then called snap elections for February 2021.

The thirty-eight-year-old Osmani formed her own party, Guxo (To Dare), and allied with Kurti's party, which was further left. As in her previous campaigns, she faced recurrent sexist attacks for her appearance, weight, and clothing, as well as false allegations about her family's ties to Serbia, from LDK leaders and others. A large turnout from youth and women helped Osmani to come in second. The Kurti-Osmani coalition won in a landslide as the old-school parties were trounced, with the LDK losing half of its seats.

EXPANDING DEMOCRACY BY ADVANCING JUSTICE AND WOMEN'S RIGHTS

The elections marked a leap ahead for women in positions of power, including a record number of women legislators, who now accounted for one-third of parliament. Six of fifteen cabinet ministers were women, including the foreign minister and the justice minister, and two women were selected as deputy prime ministers. Osmani won more votes than any other candidate. She credited the younger generation and heralded these breakthroughs for women: "It was a decision of the people of Kosovo . . . that shows that the people really want to move on. Oftentimes, I think that they're moving faster than political parties themselves, who stay quite conservative in terms of offering more opportunity—equal opportunities—to women."

The government launched a reform agenda that achieved numerous successes. The government adopted a national anti-corruption strategy and a rule of law strategy and action plan in 2021, and in 2022 the parliament passed an anti-corruption law that created an independent corruption agency overseen by the president. The wide-ranging law also established investigative powers and whistleblower protections, along with detailed standards of conduct for public officials. Osmani personally led the promulgation in 2022 of a five-year national strategy to prevent violence against women.

Despite these gains, even as president, Osmani continued to confront sexism and misogyny, including a constant stream of abuse and death threats on social media platforms such as Facebook and X, including on her official accounts. Rival politicians openly derided her appearance and belittled her standing to serve as president. "You will have to pay a price every day. It doesn't end with you becoming president," she said.

For Osmani, the fight for gender equality was an integral part of Kosovo becoming a democracy and a country of laws. It was a central part of her mission as a politician. Her country had graphically demonstrated how violence against women and denial of their rights were the most reliable predictors of a country's dysfunction, making it less stable, less prosperous, and more prone to engaging in interstate conflict. "You can never have sustainable, successful solutions without making sure that the voices of women are heard," Osmani said. "And not just heard, that they are part of the solution, that they implement that solution."

Osmani was determined to advance justice for women who had been victims of wartime violence. Women activists had been fighting for decades in the nonviolent liberation movement, in the negotiation and state-building process, and continued to demand justice for an estimated ten to twenty thousand rapes committed by Serbian forces during the 1999 war in Kosovo. With her support, the parliament passed a law in 2014 to provide a 230-euro monthly pension for rape survivors, but the social stigma deterred all but a few hundred from coming forward to undergo the intensive documentation process required to establish the crime and receive the payment.[3]

Domestic violence against women was endemic. "Kosovo has enacted some of the most advanced legislation not just in the Western Balkans but in Europe," Osmani noted. But "many of these institutions are lagging behind what these strategies are asking them to do." For those with the courage to report the crime, despite a clear criminal code and sentencing guidelines, judges and prosecutors failed to implement them. After two men killed their wives within five days in April 2024, Osmani declared a day of mourning. As the details emerged, she was furious to find out that that one of the suspects had been previously convicted of violence, but the judge had levied a fine instead of jailing him as the law required. "This is equal to an act of terrorism," Osmani said, "because the victims of domestic violence face everyday terror."[4]

She demanded that the legislature take urgent action, within weeks, to increase sentences and disciplinary sanctions for judges and prosecutors who ignored the law. She took this as a test of her presidency. "Ultimately, these positions will mean nothing if we can't use them for the benefit of all of the people and to also deal with the daily discrimination that women face in their lives, at work, in the streets, at home, or elsewhere." Women's vulnerability was increased by their economic dependence; despite Kosovo's laws guaranteeing equal inheritance, most women were bypassed in family wills, remained dependent on their spouses, and were less likely to be employed.

Osmani also believed women's leadership was vital to promoting peace in Kosovo and the Western Balkans. To that end, Kosovo promulgated a national action plan to increase the number of women serving in the police, the army, and the justice sector, and in decision-making roles throughout government. In a global conference held in Pristina in April 2024, Osmani announced the formation of a regional center of excellence for women, peace, and security in partnership with the U.S. State Department. Osmani envisioned this center becoming an important venue for regional training and action to overcome the fractious issues that made the Western Balkans the most unstable region of Europe. "Not to oversimplify things, but I think there is an opportunity . . . to be a shining example."

Women activists and politicians had been in the forefront of the efforts to move ahead from the bitter wars of the 1990s that affected the entire region. Osmani pointed to regular dialogues between women parliamentarians from Serbia and Kosovo in which she had participated as an important channel in that most conflicted bilateral relationship. "The conversation is easier [among women]," she said. "There's no swearing. There are no personal attacks." A critical mass of women leaders had been slowly forming in Kosovo and throughout the

Western Balkans to push for the resolution of conflicts, government reforms, and increased representation. Kosovo's first president, Atifete Jahaga, remained active in the fight for justice for women survivors of wartime rape, and other women were elected heads of state or government in Bosnia, Croatia, Serbia, Slovenia, and North Macedonia.

FOREIGN POLICY LEADERSHIP TO DEFEND KOSOVO AGAINST SERBIA'S DESTABILIZATION

As president, Osmani traveled constantly as Kosovo's ambassador to the world to nurture and expand the country's diplomatic relations and membership in international organizations. She reinforced ties with more than one hundred countries that recognize Kosovo and cultivated new formal relations, mostly recently with Kenya in 2025. Osmani also supported Kosovo's participation in two hundred international organizations and pressed for admission to others.[5] In 2024, Kosovo gained associate membership in NATO's parliamentary assembly. However, the stumbling block to full international recognition was Serbia, which with Russian and Chinese support continued to block Kosovo from becoming a UN member. To shine a light on its exclusion, Osmani visited New York during the annual UN gathering to meet with member states, and she traveled to annual NATO summits to thank member countries for their continued support for the UN peacekeeping force.

The ongoing conflict between Serbia and Kosovo lay at the heart of Kosovo's stalled progress. Until that conflict was resolved, Kosovo would be locked out of the United Nations and the EU. Years of negotiations mediated by the EU had produced successive agreements that ran aground in the implementation. The 2013 Brussels Agreement was superseded by the 2023 Brussels Agreement and an implementation plan.[6] Trade, recognition of license plates, and a few other terms had been implemented, but Serbia, for example, continued to episodically halt cars bearing Kosovo license plates at its border.

In her first speech as president, Osmani called for a "just and equal" approach to resolving the conflict.[7] She maintained that the EU was not holding Serbia to the terms of the Brussels Agreement, which required Serbia to grant Kosovo de facto recognition and not block its accession to international bodies; in return, Kosovo had agreed, albeit reluctantly, to create an association for the majority Serbian municipalities in northern Kosovo. In the absence of progress, tensions steadily escalated. Serbia encouraged ethnic Serbs in Kosovo to boycott elections and service in Kosovo's police force; it also supported them through jobs and "parallel institutions" like banks, post offices, and other services. Kosovo viewed this as interference in its internal affairs and installed ethnic Albanians as mayors in rerun elections. Violence broke out in 2023 as thirty NATO peacekeepers were injured in riots and further violence was instigated by a close ally of Serbia's president and the leader of the Kosovo Serbian List party, who then fled to Serbia.

Osmani had worked to return the Visoki Dečani monastery property in Kosovo to the Serbian Orthodox Church, as stipulated under the Brussels agreement, in hopes that it would gain Kosovo's admission to the Council of Europe and, along with it, access to the European human rights commission. In April 2024, the Council's parliamentary assembly voted overwhelmingly to recommend that the Council's Committee of Ministers vote to admit Kosovo.[8] Amid heavy lobbying by Serbia and Russia, however, the Council deferred its vote, asking that Kosovo first form the required Association of Serbian Municipalities.[9] Serbia suffered no penalty for opposing Kosovo's bid for membership or for its role in arming and supporting paramilitary groups. Emboldened, the Serbian president and his foreign minister declared they would never recognize Kosovo.

Prime Minister Kurti was equally intransigent. After he refused EU and U.S. requests to deescalate tensions in northern Kosovo, the EU suspended high-level contacts and financial aid. Kurti banned the use of Serbian currency in northern Kosovo and closed Serbian banks and post offices located there. He also vowed to unilaterally open the Mitrovica bridge into Serbia, which had previously been a flashpoint of tension. The EU and the United States both issued sternly worded rebukes, jeopardizing the good relations that Osmani had been working to build.

MITIGATING A DETERIORATING SITUATION

While Osmani did not break publicly with Kurti, his aggressive actions had alienated key allies. Kosovo depended heavily on U.S. and European economic and diplomatic support, and their mounting criticism of the government caused anxiety in Pristina. The EU's criticism and withholding of aid seemed one-sided to Albanian Kosovars as Serbia was actively interfering in Kosovo's sovereignty, elections, and the effective functioning of its government and economy. For years the U.S. and European governments sought to lure Serbia out of Russia's orbit. Serbia had been granted EU candidate status, though it was far from meeting the rule of law, corruption, and press freedom standards to warrant accession.

Osmani made frequent visits to the United States and Europe, seeking to conduct damage control. She visited the NATO summit in Washington and gave several speeches thanking the members for their pivotal role in protecting Kosovo and its continuing peacekeeping mission. She also visited West Point and shared Christmas dinner with NATO peacekeepers at Camp Bondsteel in Kosovo. Following the 2024 U.S. elections, she sought to build ties to the Trump administration, meeting with the deputy secretary of state and members of Congress from both parties and attending a dinner Trump held at the UN.

Everywhere she went, Osmani explained the situation from Kosovo's perspective. Kosovo remained committed to the Brussels Agreement, but she argued that Kosovo should not be under EU sanctions while Serbia sent arms into Kosovo and harbored those charged with crimes. She argued for parallel implementation of the accord's ten articles, saying "There's no cherry picking in an agreement." She also explained Kosovo's concern that Serbia would use the Association of Serbian and Minority Municipalities to undermine the country's sovereignty and stability, just as the creation of the Republika Srpska had continued to destabilize Bosnia-Herzegovina. "Kosovo undertook the ASMM as an international obligation, and we will implement it," Osmani said.

Kosovo's constitution, Osmani noted, provides more guarantees for minorities that any other constitution in the world. Ethnic Serbs are guaranteed a minimum of ten seats in the parliament, along with another ten for other minorities. Minorities are allotted two cabinet posts and representation in local government and police forces. The police commander is required to be Serbian in the areas of their majority. Education is provided in Serbian where the language predominates, and Serbian is one of two official languages. Municipalities control their budgets, including the principal public services of primary health care and education.[10]

"The way to integrate the Serb community in Kosovo is very simple, to use the constitutionally protected rights that the Constitution of Kosovo offers, without interference by Vučić," she said. "That's the way we actually did it for many, many years, until Vučić came along and started using different tactics. Which, of course, is mainly fear and terror and intimidation and violence. . . . He's sending transnational criminal organized crime groups to not just commit terrorist attacks in Kosovo, but also attack Serb citizens of Kosovo, and terrorize them by burning down their cars and houses and terrifying their kids."

Osmani said that Kosovo was committed to forming the association, but it would serve as a coordinating body, in accordance with Kosovo's constitution and as previously agreed with the former EU negotiator Federica Mogherini and the U.S. State Department Counselor Derek Chollet. Creating a higher-level body was a bad idea, she believed, because "the association, instead of giving more rights to the Serbs in the municipalities, takes rights from the citizens in the municipalities and gives them to an entity above them. That's never a good idea. It's even against the Council of Europe principles, which are intending to empower the citizen with more sovereignty, rather than vice versa."

OSMANI'S LEGACY AND THE LIMITS OF POWER IN A DUAL EXECUTIVE SYSTEM

Osmani's intensive diplomacy to articulate Kosovo's positions with supporting arguments based on international law, precedent, and mutual interests yielded progress when the EU agreed to gradually lift the sanctions on Kosovo to incentivize it to deescalate the situation in northern Kosovo.[11] The EU also commended the country's progress on judicial reform and the fight against corruption and included Kosovo in a six-billion-euro fund to spur Balkan progress toward a regional and European common market. The EU had become Kosovo's largest trade partner, investor, and provider of financial assistance since it signed a Stabilization and Association Agreement. Kosovo had received almost five hundred million euros in development projects and visa-free travel in the EU as of 2024. The United States, its top donor, had provided one billion dollars in aid since the 1999 war. Kaja Kallas's arrival as High Representative for Security and Foreign Policy brought the first Eastern European perspective to that office. Kallas appreciated Kosovo's concerns about Russia's involvement in the Western Balkans.

Serbia was also rocked by mass anti-corruption protests, the first since Vučić came to power. But Kosovo's outlook remained tenuous as the Trump administration cut aid to Kosovo as part of its drastic dismantling of support for democracy, development, and women. Kurti failed to win a majority in February 2025 elections and became a caretaker prime minister for most of the year.

Osmani would likely remain a leading figure in Kosovo politics, even if she chose not to run for reelection in 2026. Her tireless diplomacy significantly raised Kosovo's profile and increased its ties with other countries and international organizations. She supported equality, regional peace, and reforms to advance Kosovo's EU application. She argued for an even-handed approach to ending the conflict with Serbia amid growing frustration among Kosovars. She navigated the limitations of a dual executive system, seeking to temper the negative effects of her governing partner's actions.

Osmani's tenure demonstrated her ability to navigate complex international security and diplomatic crises and served as a role model for future aspiring women leaders. Her competence in foreign affairs, law, and diplomacy and her forceful leadership clearly broke the masculine stereotype and showed a woman capable of leading on the world stage; Kosovo's younger generation firmly validated that view. Her legacy would center around her unstinting defense of diplomacy and peaceful means to resolve conflict. "What I've learned during the past twenty-five years in politics and in Kosovo's institutions—and what I think Kosovo as a country has learned—is that our strength lies in the power of our partnerships," she said. Osmani nurtured those partnerships, including with Slovenia's first woman president, Nataša Pirc Musar, who was a strong ally in the search for peace in the Western Balkans.

Chapter Nine

NATAŠA PIRC MUSAR

REDUCING CONFLICT AT HOME AND ABROAD

SINCE ITS INDEPENDENCE IN 1991, Slovenia had been an island of stability in the restive Western Balkans, until it became destabilized by the rise of an autocratic populist, Janez Janša, who aligned with Hungary's Viktor Orbán. Elected for a third time as prime minister in 2020, Janša sharply escalated his use of state powers to attack political rivals, the justice system, and the press.[1] Sustained mass protests broke out to counter the authoritarian turn, and a coalition led by the newly formed Freedom Movement won the 2022 elections. Robert Golob, a businessman, was elected prime minister and Nataša Pirc Musar, a human rights lawyer, the country's first woman president. Pirc Musar sought to use her status as an independent and the largely symbolic powers of her office to address the country's deep polarization and promote reforms to the social safety net and gender equality. Abroad, she worked to resolve the Western Balkans conflict and to champion democracy, women's leadership, and digital safety in global forums.

FROM JOURNALISM TO PUBLIC SERVICE

Motorcycle-riding Nataša Pirc Musar inherited an independent streak from her parents, factory workers who eschewed party membership even though it was the way to get ahead in communist Yugoslavia. She did not imagine a life in politics and entered journalism instead. She gained national visibility as a television anchor at age twenty-four and was later offered the position of information commissioner, a quasi-independent position overseeing the release of public information and protection of data privacy rights. The position provided the opportunity to expand the former socialist country's appreciation of the public's right to know and the benefits of transparency in government. In her bid to become general manager of the national broadcasting company, Pirc Musar faced pressure from politicians to appoint their nominees to jobs. She refused and was denied the position, after which she opened a law practice specializing in media, privacy law, and human rights. Pirc Musar also provided expert advice to organizations and countries as the EU drafted and enacted its landmark General Data Protection Regulation.

THE CAMPAIGN TO REVERSE DEMOCRATIC BACKSLIDING

Like many Slovenians, Pirc Musar grew concerned about the country's trajectory as the country's leading conservative politician, Janez Janša, steadily eroded Slovenia's democratic norms over three terms as prime minister. He became increasingly extreme, riding the anti-immigrant, right-wing populist wave sweeping Central Europe into a second and then a third term in office, despite being convicted on bribery charges in 2013.

Janša had built a web of political organizations in addition to the Slovenian Democratic Party of Slovenia (SDS) that he ran with an iron fist for thirty years, supported by numerous media outlets funded by Orbán's network in Hungary. In daily social media attacks, Janša propagated conspiracy theories and targeted politicians and female journalists, whom he called "prostitutes" and other sexist names. In 2020, Janša began a campaign against the media for its "monopoly of lies" and halted funding to the state news agency. He pressured the main weekly to fire its director on trumped-up charges and gave contracts to the top private Czech-owned television station in exchange for favorable coverage. Government funding was redirected to conservative outlets.

When Slovenia assumed the rotating European Council presidency, Janša declared that his top priority would be combatting left-wing extremism. In addition to mimicking Trump's language and creating its own "Slovenia First" label, the SDS amplified neo-Nazi and identitarian groups such as Generation Identity Slovenia, publishing and promoting the latter's manifesto. International criticism of his government grew, as the Council of Europe and the U.S. State Department expressed concern about the erosion of rights, and Freedom House named Slovenia as experiencing the most severe decline of any European country.[2]

Claiming that communist elites had taken over the government and civil institutions, Janša used his powers to investigate opposition parties and cut funding to NGOs and cultural institutions. Defending clients against Janša's suits, Pirc Musar saw the weaponization of government powers firsthand. "I realized how Mr. Janša was abusing his power and that his way was to be hostile toward those who do not agree with him."[3] Pirc Musar became increasingly troubled not only by the erosion of civil rights but also by the toxic culture of division, slander, and hate tearing at her bucolic alpine country of lakes, forests, and castles. She firmly believed that a representative democracy needed parties across the spectrum, including on the right, but not hostile, extremist, radical parties like the one Janša now led. She understood the role that mass migration had played in stirring up unrest as governments failed to deliver adequate responses. As president of the Red Cross in Slovenia, she had seen the deluge up close. "I was watching 15,000 people per day crossing the border from Croatia to Slovenia, offering them help," she recalled. "[The European Union] left those countries completely alone to deal with hundreds of thousands of migrants a day." The massive wave of migration had caused many European countries to experience an upsurge in support for right-wing extremism, as people fell prey to fearmongering. She sympathized with their concerns about jobs and public order, but not the xenophobia that had gripped her country and much of Europe.

As Janša ruled increasingly by executive order, gutting the judicial system and attacking trade unions and rights organizations, mass protests mounted. One of the leading protest organizers was the 8th of March Institute, a women's and civil rights organization led by Nika Kovač. She had excelled at bringing diverse groups together around numerous causes such as environmental preservation, anti-bullying campaigns, and a "get out and vote" effort for the 2022 campaign. Kovač solicited citizens to submit antidemocratic laws they wanted to overturn, and her group selected fifteen to form the core of their campaign. After Kovač received death threats and the Janša government accused her of waging an illegal electoral campaign, a group of women lawyers including Pirc Musar represented her.[4]

The mass mobilization produced a 70 percent turnout, and the Freedom Movement won the parliamentary elections in April 2022. Commentators declared the end of the Janša era, but his party still came in second given the fractured landscape of upstart parties. It was a vote for democracy, nonetheless: The Freedom Movement went from two seats to forty-one. Its leader Robert Golob, formerly the head of a state-owned green energy company, formed a coalition with Social Democrats and the Left party and became prime minister in May.

VICTORIES FOR WOMEN'S LEADERSHIP

Pirc Musar decided that her career of defending civil and political rights and her public profile as an independent were valuable assets that could help bring the fractured country together. She threw her hat in the ring when the presidential elections were announced and won the endorsement of two former presidents, Milan Kučan and Danilo Türk. Her chief opponent on the right was Janša's former foreign minister, Anže Logar; five other candidates ran from the left. Announcing her candidacy, she pledged if elected to "dedicate my presidency to climate change, gender equality, the fight against hate speech, media freedom, disinformation and the impact of technology on privacy."[5]

Pirc Musar faced an uphill battle because she did not have a party structure behind her candidacy and registry requirements for independent candidates were onerous. She was gratified when 450 friends and acquaintances volunteered in two days. She considered her main assets to be national name recognition and her familiarity with the media, but she was shocked and hurt by the harsh, ad hominem insults she received in the press and online. She was called fat, ugly, old, and other names, in an avalanche of sexist abuse that none of the male candidates received. Her husband, Aleš Musar, tried to stop her from looking at the social media and press coverage. He also became a target of scrutiny around his wealth and use of tax havens. While her husband defended himself in the press, Pirc Musar tried to focus her campaign on the pressing issues facing the country.

In the first round of voting, Pirc Musar placed second behind the leading contender, Janša's former foreign minister Logar. Golob and the parties on the left endorsed her, and she won the runoff election in December 2022, besting Logar 54 to 46 percent.

The successful mass protest movement to restore democracy had ushered in new faces, including more women than ever before. Slovenians not only elected Pirc Musar as their first woman president but also elected a record number of women to parliament, increasing their share from 27 to 41 percent of the seats, and selected a woman as speaker for the first time. Tanja Fajon, head of the Social Democrats, became the first woman to serve as the country's foreign minister. Slovenia also achieved another gender equality milestone with strong support from Pirc Musar, who had long defended gay rights. The high court overturned the Janša-era law that defined marriage as only between a man and a woman, and despite vociferous protests from Janša's party, the parliament then passed a law allowing same-sex couples to marry and adopt—the first post-socialist country to do so—with wide popular support. By contrast, Hungarian law prohibits even discussing homosexuality in front of children. Pirc Musar gave an enthusiastic speech and marched in the Pride Month parade, raising the pride flag at the presidential palace next to the Slovenian flag.

Pirc Musar worked with Prime Minister Golob, Foreign Minister Tanja Fajon (who led the Social Democratic party), and House Speaker Urška Klakočar Zupančič to support legislation restoring editorial independence and funding to the state broadcast and news agencies and establishing new rules for board appointments and government oversight. Democracy watchers praised Slovenia's quick reversal of the backsliding that had occurred under Janša. Pirc Musar held no illusions that much remained to be done to address the deeper sources of divisions and unmet needs that had been exploited in the Janša era. The divides were political, generational, and rural/urban. Some disputes went back to World War II; others revolved around taxes and gaps in health care and pensions for older Slovenians. As an independent, she believed she could reach across the polarized society and connect with young and old, conservative and liberal Slovenians through new civic projects and advocacy of better social welfare policies and programs.

USING LIMITED PRESIDENTIAL POWERS TO STRENGTHEN DEMOCRACY

Pirc Musar came into office determined to use the limited powers available to her. She understood that soft power would be as important as her specifically defined powers. As head of state, she represented the country internationally, served as commander in chief of the armed forces, and nominated the Constitutional Court judges. Understanding the power of communication, Pirc Musar saw that the largely ceremonial office of the president could be a powerful vehicle to articulate urgent and long-term priorities for the nation, promote democratic and civic culture, and galvanize international action on climate change, women's leadership, and responsible digital and global governance.

The president also had the power to propose initiatives, call elections, and declare states of emergency. Through initiatives she could use the presidency's influence, visibility, and bully pulpit to help steer the country out of division and focus it on critical national, regional, and global issues. Her predecessor had said little and done less during his ten years in office to deter Janša's attacks on Slovenian democratic institutions and civil discourse. "My first task will be to open a dialogue among all Slovenians," she said in her first remarks as president-elect. "It is the duty of the president to speak out when human rights are violated, when hate speech overrides respectful speech, when the constitution and the law are violated, when the welfare state is collapsing, and democracy has its wings clipped."

Pirc Musar relied heavily on her convening power to bring in young, old, disaffected, and disconnected Slovenians with innovative, uplifting events. On Slovenia's annual statehood day, she staged a gala performance in Ljubljana's main park, an avant-garde work of song, dance, and video art around the theme of climate change and the need for environmental actions to protect Slovenia's alpine beauty. Jane Goodall made a guest video appearance. In her speech, Pirc Musar implored Slovenians to overcome their longest-standing rift, between descendants of Slovenians who had sided with the Nazis and those of communist Partisans during and after World War II. For decades the country had been torn over demands to establish a memorial for those killed by the victors, many of whose remains were still buried in the forests, and the lack of accountability for war crimes on both sides.

Pirc Musar had no shortage of ideas for her five-year term and tackled her planning just as energetically as she had built her law firm, with the most competent lawyers she could find, who happened to be women. She brought Ula Tomaduz, one of her firm's rising stars, to serve as her chief of cabinet. Tomaduz, who had pursued academic and legal work on women's rights, provided advice on those issues. Pirc Musar held her first of a series of strategic forums on the issue of health and pension reform, as the two most pressing issues affecting the population. She opened the palace to a wide variety of guests, with a steady stream of events to honor local community workers and activists. She formed a kitchen cabinet of official and academic experts to advise her on various domestic and international issues and was the first Slovenian president to craft a formal strategy for what she hoped to accomplish. Given that her powers were largely symbolic, it was important to plan how to marshal the public spotlight, her convening power, her official travel abroad, and her power of appointment for maximum effect.

Her primary goal was to use the presidential platform to defend democratic values, the rule of law, and human rights to revive Slovenia's constitutional democracy and its past reputation as a cornerstone of stable democracy in the Western Balkans. She used educational and cultural events and speeches to bring Slovenians together. She also pressed for women's leadership as an integral part of democracy. She had cofounded an organization called She Knows to promote women experts as public speakers, maintaining an online roster so that no conference organizer or television station would lack for women experts to call. In a podcast series she started as well as the annual Bled Strategic Forum, she featured women leaders such as the European human rights commissioner, top Slovenian scholars, and the democracy activists Sviatlana Tsiaknouskaya of Belarus and Yulia Navalnaya, widow of Russian opposition leader Andrei Navalny, who was poisoned, jailed, and ultimately murdered by Putin.

FOSTERING PEACE IN THE WESTERN BALKANS

On the international front, Pirc Musar took on the festering Western Balkans conflict. Tensions were rising in the region, and many countries' bid for EU memberships had stalled over the previous twelve years. Russia used its influence to support Serbia and increase regional instability as a wedge to weaken Europe. Slovenia was ideally positioned to help as it had not suffered the same ethnic conflict as its neighbors, and Pirc Musar had a ready vehicle. Her predecessor had founded the Brdo-Brijuni process, a joint Slovenian-Croatian initiative, in 2010 to strengthen mutual trust and cooperation among the Western Balkan countries and help advance their accession to the European Union.

Pirc Musar faced reluctance among her neighbors as rising tensions had marred recent summits. At the 2021 gathering, no declaration was issued because of a dispute between Croatia and Bosnia-Herzegovina. In 2022, bitter recriminations between Serbia and Kosovo resulted in a watered-down compromise statement.[6] Both Serbia and Croatia were not inclined to meet, but Pirc Musar traveled to meet with each leader in the region to make her case. She had a cordial closed-door meeting with Serbian President Vučić, but she was put on the spot at the concluding press conference. Asked about protests and press freedoms in Serbia, she gave her usual strong defense of civil rights and did not mince words about the tensions. "Serbia and Kosovo should find a solution to ease the tensions. The current situation does not help the EU or either country. The whole Western Balkan region is not progressing fast enough. I see a lack of political will."[7]

Pirc Musar persuaded her Croatian cofounder by proposing that the group focus on common issues, such as EU integration, the emigration of their young people for better opportunities elsewhere, and the need for faster adaptation to climate change. The group convened in 2023 in Skopje and acknowledged the urgent need to accelerate reforms to gain EU accession and counteract their populations' increasing pessimism about the prospects. The next year Pirc Musar again convened the summit, but the violence that had broken out in Kosovo had brought the region to the most delicate moment since the end of the war. Russia was actively stirring the pot. Pirc Musar warned, "Other stakeholders are jumping in, like Russia and China. If the European Union wants to stay strong, we need to speed up the process. [I would] decisively ask Vučić, do you want to join the BRICS or do you want to join the EU?"[8] At the meeting in Montenegro, she pledged that as EU members, Slovenia and Croatia would press inside the organization for the EU to prioritize accession talks. The summit devolved as countries leveled barbs at Serbia. The Bosnian leader said that the region's leaders had to decide whether they supported the EU or Russia and that those "who accept Russia's attitude toward its neighbors that leads to unhappiness and tragedy."[9] Vučić retorted that those who profit economically from Serbia should not criticize it.

Pirc Musar tried to steer her counterparts back to their common goal. "Progress towards EU membership is slowing, while the challenges facing an incomplete European Union continue to grow," she said.[10] She reminded them that 4.8 million young people had left the Balkans in recent years, a sign of their faltering hope in the region's prospects for peace and progress. The Baltics had progressed much further and faster since the Soviet Union's breakup. In the end, the group reaffirmed their commitment to domestic reforms, local integration, and energy transition. Meeting the EU deadline for climate neutrality by 2050 would require significant action by the coal-dependent region.[11]

The nudges from all sides produced revived action on EU enlargement after twelve years of stasis. Ursula von der Leyen, the newly reelected European Commission president, prioritized EU enlargement, pledged to reform the accession process, and increased assistance to help candidate states to meet the requirements. Negotiations accelerated in late 2024 as Albania formally opened talks. Kosovo held only potential candidate status, but it had moved ahead with reforms. Pirc Musar visited Osmani in Kosovo and continued to engage with her other counterparts in the region; she also enlisted the support of former heads of state who had founded the Brdo-Brijuni process to overcome the roadblocks to integration and stability in the region.

ADVANCING A GLOBAL AGENDA OF UN REFORM AND WOMEN'S LEADERSHIP

Beyond her efforts to restore Slovenia's democratic culture and reduce conflict in the Western Balkans, Pirc Musar used her role as head of state to promote reforms on the international stage. During its two-year term on the UN Security Council from 2024 to 2026, Slovenia organized sessions on global governance reform, conflict prevention, and climate change. In her first appearance at the UN General Assembly in September 2023, Pirc Musar called for the UN Security Council to expand its membership, curtail the five permanent members' use of the veto, and heed repeated calls to refrain from vetoes in cases of mass atrocities. Pressure from General Assembly debates and from countries including Slovenia led to passage of ceasefire resolutions on Gaza.[12]

Pirc Musar also pressed the case for the inclusion of digital safety in the UN Global Digital Compact and legislation. She urged tech companies to "take more systematic responsibility for the content they host and moderate. They should better protect users from hate speech, disinformation, and other harmful online content. What is unacceptable offline should not be acceptable online."[13] She called the marginalization of women and girls "a monumental waste of potential for our societies" and urged that the UN select a woman as its next secretary-general.[14]

Throughout 2024, Pirc Musar traveled to press the case for UN reform, digital safety, and women's leadership in various forums. She returned to the UN dais in 2025 to make a bold call to end the war in Gaza, declaring, "We did not stop the Holocaust, we did not stop the genocide in Rwanda, we did not stop the genocide in Srebrenica. We must stop the genocide in Gaza. There are no excuses any more, none!" The Slovenian government had recognized Palestine in June, and the UK, France, Canada, and Australia did so in the fall, making a total of 160 countries recognizing Palestine as a measure to stop the war and defend Palestine's right to exist.

These actions did not lead to immediate breakthroughs, but they were part of the patient work of diplomacy. The dual executive system of government limited what Pirc Musar could achieve as the less powerful member of the duo. She sought to exercise the powers that she did have, and frictions with Prime Minister Golob arose as he disagreed with some of her appointments, her invitations to foreign leaders, and her public support for a minister's rights after he fired her.[15] After Golob called a referendum on Slovenia's membership in NATO, Pirc Musar sought to calm the waters, telling the European Parliament that Slovenia remained committed to the European security community and an anchor in peacekeeping efforts. The country's democracy recovery remained fragile: Janša's party won the most seats in the 2024 elections for the European Parliament, raising the prospect that it could return to power.

Despite the tensions with Golob, Pirc Musar had demonstrated how to leverage the powers of the presidency to create visibility, support, and momentum for democracy, civility, and gender equality. Deft use of symbolic powers could move important projects forward, as another feminist human rights lawyer, Mary Robinson, had done as president of Ireland, to advance gender equality at home and bring global attention to famine in Somalia and the Northern Ireland conflict. Their examples provide useful guides for future women leaders in countries with dual national executives on ways to convert presidential posts into real sources of influence and power.

Chapter Ten

MIA AMOR MOTTLEY

ADVANCING CLIMATE JUSTICE AND INTERNATIONAL REFORM

IN 2018, Mia Amor Mottley became the first woman to serve as prime minister of Barbados; during her tenure, she advanced the country's democracy and gender equality. She confronted dire threats to her country's viability: the mounting damage of climate change and a debt burden that hobbled its ability to recover. Mottley fought for financial reforms that would benefit Barbados and the debt-laden Global South. She persuaded the World Bank to grant debt suspension clauses to help countries struck by climate-related natural disasters, advanced new debt-for-credit swaps, and helped create a loss-and-damage fund to provide grants for recovery. Her Bridgetown Initiative for climate finance reform won support from developed countries, international banks, private creditors, and philanthropies like the Rockefeller Foundation. She also lobbied for wider reform of the global governance system.

ENCOUNTERING SEXISM IN
THE CONTEST FOR POWER

Mottley became prime minister in May 2018 after years of struggle against sexism in politics. Her victory was complete, as her Labour Party swept all thirty seats in parliament. She was born into a political family: Her grandfather had been mayor of Bridgetown, the capital, and a member of parliament like her father, who was also a diplomat.[1] After graduating with a law degree from the London School of Economics in 1986, Mottley became the youngest ever Queen's Counsel in Barbados. She ran for parliament in 1991 but lost. She won her next race in 1994 and was named minister for education, youth, and culture at age twenty-nine. She continued her ascent, serving as attorney general and then the first woman deputy prime minister from 2003 to 2008. Mottley did not just notch victories but made a name as a reformer. As education minister, she launched an ambitious program to refurbish schools, install digital infrastructure, and improve training for teachers and administrators. She also gained experience in national security and economic development roles, helping the Caribbean regional organization CARICOM to form a telecom single market.

Despite her political pedigree, Mottley's ascent was marked by bruising and personal battles, both within her party and outside it. She was a rare female in a male-dominated political scene that turned ugly as she neared the top. Her party turned to her as leader after it was ousted from power in 2008, but the former prime minister staged a comeback in 2010, orchestrating a no-confidence vote against her. She regained the party leadership three years later, but the 2018 elections were marked by a dirty campaign of sexist innuendo against her. The opposition speaker of parliament and a minister sought to defame her as a single woman, calling on her to declare her sexual orientation.

Mottley also faced sexism in her own party, which purged all but four women from the leadership council when she was voted out. She denounced widespread male domination of party politics in a 2011 speech at the Organization of the American States, saying, "Until you can democratize the political parties and the institutions in which these women participate, there will not be the opportunity for women truly to have an equal chance." As attorney general, she advocated for HIV care and gay rights, but the socially conservative island remained hostile to gays. It retained a harsh colonial-era law imposing life imprisonment for consensual same-sex relations and no provision for same-sex unions.

CRISIS MANAGEMENT: MEETING THE DEBT CRISIS

In her first days as prime minister, Mottley discovered that the country was teetering on the brink of insolvency. Twenty-eight days of reserves remained to pay government bills, and the government, she discovered, carried the third-highest debt burden per capita in the world. The previous government had taken out commercial loans that had ballooned as the debts were packaged, sold, and resold to other banks and private equity funds in an opaque market.

Mottley called the International Monetary Fund (IMF) and insisted on speaking with its head, Christine Lagarde. Without an emergency agreement with the IMF, Mottley would be unable to renegotiate the terms of its debt and would be forced to default. "We will raise taxes and cut the budget, but we need to have a breather," Mottley told her.[2] Much to her surprise, Lagarde agreed. Mottley began an arduous negotiation with the country's creditors that lasted for months. She insisted on a longer term and a lower interest rate to avoid plunging the country deeper into debt. In the end, Mottley won a deal that reduced the debt burden by one-quarter and lowered the interest rate from 7 to 3 percent.

Mottley also held out for another important concession. Barbados sits at the easternmost edge of the Caribbean, where several Atlantic hurricanes lash its powdery white beaches every year. For years she had watched the shoreline in front of her family's house erode and tons of sargassum wash up from the warming seas. Hotels were forced to hire trucks to clear beaches each day at a cost of up to a million dollars per square kilometer.[3] The fishing industry, other livelihoods, and lives were increasingly jeopardized by extreme weather. Yet Barbados paid more in debt service than rebuilding and refitting the country for worsening storms. So Mottley insisted on a novel hurricane clause that allowed the country to pause payments in the event of a natural disaster. That would give Barbados breathing room for the costs of rebuilding. In return, she agreed to tighten the government's belt dramatically to achieve a 6 percent surplus each year until the debt fell to 50 percent of GDP, from

175 percent. That would entail stiff cuts, but it was worth it to avoid increasing the debt.

The experience shook Mottley deeply. How many other countries, she wondered, were in this predicament? She retained the finance ministry portfolio to ensure that Barbados executed the deal, and with the help of her adviser Avinash Persaud, an economist and former banker, she began to delve into the intricacies of global finance. In the space of a decade, developing countries had gone from being net recipients of financing to paying out billions of dollars every year. The entire developing world was caught in rapidly escalating debt service—the poorest countries as well as the middle-income countries where 70 percent of the poor people lived. Barbados, one of the latter, was paying more than half its GDP to service its debt. They were trapped in short-term, high-interest debt, more than half of it owed to private lenders and hedge funds that reaped windfall profits via escalating interest rates. During the pandemic, as interest rates hit a twenty-year high, poor countries paid out over a trillion dollars a year to service their debts.

That left the developing world without funds to invest in health, education, and recovery from the mounting costs of climate change. Island countries like Barbados were experiencing more climate damage each year, not only from more frequent devastating storms but from the gradual but equally ruinous effects of rising sea levels. Small island developing states (SIDS) were becoming less habitable as land eroded, droughts increased, and salt water invaded the water supply. Countries had no money to invest in rebuilding homes, infrastructure, and businesses that could survive the next storm.

Between the global recession of 2008 and the pandemic, the SIDS' total debt had doubled. Mottley realized that only a collective effort could address this global crisis. At a UN gathering to review the SIDS ten-year plan, she said we "must recognize that we are here not just as representatives of our countries but as trustees for humanity itself."

EXPANDING DEMOCRACY AND GENDER EQUALITY

Mottley wanted to fight for more extensive financial reform and faster action on climate change, but her immediate priority was to fulfill her party's pledge to accomplish Barbados's transition to a parliamentary republic. Twenty years before, her party had promised to hold a referendum on the matter but never did. Polls showed that an overwhelming majority supported the change, so Mottley decided to skip the referendum—a controversial decision—and ask parliament to act. In her annual throne speech on September 15, 2020, she announced that Barbados would transition from a constitutional monarchy headed by Queen Elizabeth II to a parliamentary republic by the country's fifty-fifth independence anniversary in December 2021. "It is time to leave the colonial past behind," she said. She also asked the parliament to amend the constitution to remove all mentions of monarchy from the charter, which it did in June 2021.

Parliament established the office of president and elected Mottley's nominee, Dame Sandra Mason, who had served as governor-general since 2018, to the position. When Mason took office on November 30, 2021, Barbados became one of three countries to have elected women serving as both head of state and head of government. Mottley also presented a new draft constitution to parliament that, if adopted, would further expand democracy for the island by unequivocally declaring Barbadians' equality in all respects, including sex, gender, or sexual orientation. In a related step in 2022, following similar actions in two other eastern Caribbean nations, Barbados's high court struck down colonial-era antigay laws and a 1992 law that imposed a life sentence for gay men found guilty of having sex with other men.

TACKLING DEBT AND CLIMATE CHANGE

In January 2022 general elections, Mottley again won a landslide victory with all thirty seats in parliament. Armed with that strong mandate, she decided it was time to take on international financial reform and address climate change for the benefit of her country and others. Even though developing countries were still struggling with the effects of the pandemic, the financial community was bearing down on them to service their debt. The IMF was requesting that Barbados return to meeting its 6 percent budget surplus. In July, she gathered UN and IMF officials, world leaders, the Rockefeller Foundation, and the Open Society Institute for a retreat in Bridgetown.

The resulting proposal, "The Bridgetown Initiative for the Reform of the Global Financial Architecture," called for international financial institutions, developed countries, and the private sector to make major changes in financing so that developing countries could recover from climate damage and develop more resilient economies. Mottley pointed out that developed countries had historically benefited from generous financing terms: Britain had taken a century to repay its War Loan bonds from World War I, and Germany's debt payments were capped at 3.5 percent of its annual export revenues.[4] Even today, some developing countries paid 14 percent interest rates on loans while developed countries paid just 4 percent.

The Bridgetown Initiative made specific requests to every sector of the financial community. It called on the IMF to suspend interest surcharges on loans to cash-strapped developing countries and to rapidly launch its promised Resilience and Sustainability Trust. It called for developed countries to make one hundred billion dollars in interest-free IMF Special Drawing Rights (SDRs) available and for new SDRs to be issued. It called on multilateral development banks to suspend debt service payments to the poorest countries, adopt the disaster clause that Barbados had won as standard practice, and create a loss-and-damage fund to provide emergency grants to developing countries struck by climate disasters. It estimated the total funding need at one trillion dollars.

Mottley then began a global campaign to publicize and gain support for the Bridgetown Initiative. At the annual high-level UN meeting in September, she noted that developed countries had not delivered the hundred billion dollars in assistance promised at the previous climate summit. Every country had a stake in acting: The current twenty-one million climate refugees would increase to one billion by 2050. In November, at the climate summit in Egypt, Mottley and other climate activists made a loss-and-damage fund their central demand and won leaders' agreement to create such a fund.

French President Emmanuel Macron and Mottley convened a summit in Paris in June 2023 to reach a global financial pact with fifty heads of state and other leaders who were ready to take bold steps. Mottley achieved one of her top goals when the World Bank agreed to include the natural disaster "pause clause" in all its future loans. This commitment by the leading development bank was a breakthrough that created a precedent for other lenders to follow.[5]

That fall, at the climate summit in Dubai, after protracted negotiations, the countries formally established the loss-and-damage fund with initial funding pledges of $700 million. This was far below the hundred-billion-dollar goal, but it was a start. Mottley and her team realized that encouraging the world's most powerful entities to act was a long-term proposition. Her chief of the Bridgetown Initiative, Pepukaye Bardouille, had overseen her native Dominica's recovery from Hurricane Maria and was an expert in global infrastructure development from years of experience at the International Finance Corporation. Mottley and her team celebrated the achievements of the loss-and-damage fund's creation and the World Bank's adoption of debt suspension for countries struck by natural disasters, but they also knew that the scale of funding was woefully insufficient to the problem.

As it became clear that governments were unlikely to supply the sums needed, Mottley and her team fleshed out additional funding options in a new version of the Bridgetown proposal in September 2024. In addition to the requests to governments and institutional lenders, the new document proposed taxing major sources of wealth, particularly those that contributed to or benefited from climate change and the high cost of money: fossil fuel industries, high-emission activities like aviation and shipping, companies reaping financial windfalls from sky-high interest rates, the growing class of super-rich who were becoming trillionaires through the booming market, and unregulated private equity hedge funds. The model for their proposal was the U.S. Oil Spill Liability Trust Fund, which charges oil companies nine cents a barrel to finance cleanup and economic mitigation from oil spills. The new Bridgetown "global solidarity levy" would tax industries and ask billionaire philanthropists to pledge a fixed amount of their foundations' annual giving to this effort.

Mottley's strategy was to focus the world on the topline amount needed—$1.8 trillion—and then show how it could be raised by tapping a variety of sources for pennies on the dollar. She emphasized the urgency of the need, the consequences for the planet, and the costs of delay. Her stirring speeches, bold critiques, and high aspirations gained increasing attention; she was named one of *Time* magazine's 100 Most Influential People and *Forbes'* 100 Most Powerful Women and recognized by the UN Foundation's Global Leadership Award.

Mottley was also on the short list of candidates to be the next UN secretary-general. Pressure was growing for the UN to name a woman, and it was Latin America's turn in the normal geographic rotation. While she was best known for her leadership on climate change and financial reform, Mottley also strongly advocated for more democratic and representative international institutions. In a meeting at the Council on Foreign Relations, she asked with a smile, "How frank do you want me to be?" before describing the built-in legacy of inequality that remained enshrined in the structure, composition, and decision-making rules in global governance bodies. For developing countries, "it means that you don't have the capacity to change the trajectory or to change the attitude of these institutions."[6] She praised the steps the World Bank and the IMF had taken to increase the number of African countries on their boards and the growing support for increasing the number of permanent members of the UN Security Council to include the developing world. "You cannot appreciate what we're going through if you don't have knowledge or people at the table for consultation," she said. Mottley noted that the world had come together to end slavery and other ills and expressed optimism that it could do so again. "If we don't find common purpose, then I don't know what will happen to us," she said. "But I know that in the past humans did, and we can as well."

Mottley did not shrink from engaging people with different views, but rather sought to persuade them. She knew Trump did not favor bold action to address climate change, but she nonetheless framed arguments that might appeal to him. Noting his success in producing the COVID-19 vaccine, she said it "is the same warp speed that we want to encourage him and others to look at for decarbonizing technology," she said.[7] She pointed out that profits were to be made in capturing methane, a major source of emissions, for sale rather than flaring it from gas wells. Climate legislation was producing jobs in Republican districts, and climate migration would prompt massive flight from uninhabitable places. She suggested a face-to-face meeting to discuss the bold moves that could be made with Nobel Prize–worthy consequence. "Only by personal meetings among world leaders can the massive changes needed on climate action be achieved. President Trump has been very clear about the importance of that kind of face-to-face conversation in the things that he believes that he can solve as well."

BRINGING THE BENEFITS OF REFORM HOME

Critics at home complained that Mottley spent too much time abroad instead of solving their problems at home, but she was working to bring home the benefits of the reforms she had negotiated. Barbados suffered major damage when Hurricane Beryl, the earliest Category 5 hurricane of the season ever to hit the Caribbean, passed just off its shores in 2024. Homes, hotels, the harbor, and 90 percent of the fishing fleet that fed much of the population were destroyed.

Mottley delivered results for Barbados on an impressive scale. She secured a $54 million loan from the World Bank, the first the island had received from the bank in years. The loan included the two key reforms she had fought for: a clause allowing prioritization of climate-related disaster recovery over debt repayment for up to two years and a rapid response option allowing redirection of funds to emergency needs. She also secured a long-term, low-cost loan for $183 million from the IMF's Resilience and Sustainability Trust, which was now up and running. Every year, storm damage grew worse; the World Bank calculated that Barbados averaged one climate event a year with an average annual loss of $48 million.[8]

Mottley also broke new ground with the first-ever debt-for-climate-resilience swap. The deal financed a water reclamation plant that would double the island's water supply and reduce the country's debt. The deal was a model also for pooled financing, in this case from the Inter-American Development Bank, the European Investment Bank, and the Green Climate Fund. The loan replaced more expensive debt, enabling Barbados to lower its debt-to-GDP ratio to 105 percent.[9] The progress she had made in debt reduction, pension reform, and budget cuts raised the country's credit rating.

A LEGACY OF CHANGE-MAKING

Mottley had achieved signal successes: adoption of the natural disaster clause to suspend debt repayment; the creation of a loss-and-damage fund; and new financing models that pooled resources and swapped debt for investment in building resilient economies. Moreover, she had greatly raised awareness of the inequity of current financing models. The World Bank embraced Mottley's arguments in its 2024 annual report, stating, "It's time to face the reality: the poorest countries facing debt distress need debt relief if they are to have a shot at lasting prosperity." It added, "Private creditors that make risky, high-interest loans to poor countries ought to bear a fair share of the cost when the bet goes bad."[10]

Mottley had proven that a leader of a country of fewer than 300,000 people could mobilize a large, diverse, and influential coalition. She used her negotiating skills and diplomacy to seek progress through compromise. Her personal leadership style was frank but also warm; she reached out to create friendship, calling male counterparts she came to know as friend, brother, and uncle. She sought above all to be inspiring, especially to the next generation that would carry on advocacy of change. In a breezy stadium in Barbados, she commemorated the island's Independence Day and the one hundredth birthday of Shirley Chisholm, a Barbadian American who became the first black woman senator and first woman to run for president of the United States. "She achieved mighty things and laid a pathway that still waits for the full fruition of its promise," Mottley said of Chisholm, who had the courage to say, "I am good enough to be the president of the United States of America." She urged the young men and women in the stadium to "approach life with a spirit of can-do" and "choose faith over anxiety," quoting the American senator. Celebrating the country's recovery with a growth rate approaching 4 percent, Mottley exclaimed, "We are on the move now."

Mottley no doubt benefited from family ties in her ascent to power, but she overcame persistent sexism to achieve and maintain her leadership position. The skills and experience she brought to the job were forged by her own efforts. Faced with severe climate damage and inequitable access to finance, Mottley set out to change the system not only for her country but for the world. She expanded Barbados's democracy, including through promotion of gender equality. In taking an ambitious approach to governing, she served as a role model for future women leaders not to curtail their goals and to build coalitions by finding common interests, seeking compromises, and embodying an optimistic spirit of change-making.

Chapter Eleven

WOMEN AND DEMOCRACY

THE CONCEPT OF DEMOCRACY has for many decades included the idea of gender equality, including women's role in governance. This idea has been imperfectly realized owing to structural barriers, prejudice, and other reasons. But the many women leaders who have been able to overcome such impediments demonstrate that they are not just beneficiaries of democracy but contributors to it. Not all have been successful, and some have been undemocratic, but many have proven capable of governing effectively even in the most difficult of circumstances. They have fended off authoritarians, defended their countries from aggression, and strengthened their democracies. They have advanced gender equality and other reforms to create fairer and more resilient societies. By taking their places in the leadership ranks—and then delivering—they have made their countries more representative and democratic. Given the ample evidence, it is finally time to lay to rest the myth that women are not suited to govern.

HOW WOMEN RISE TO POWER

Women's opportunities to lead are affected by many variables. Among them are a country's political system, as research has demonstrated and these recent leaders' stories confirm. More women are elected in countries with parliamentary systems rather than single executive presidential systems. Women are also more likely to be elected in dual executive systems, in which power is shared between a prime minister and a president. Among the leaders discussed here, Kaja Kallas, Mia Amor Mottley, Vjosa Osmani, Nataša Pirc Musar, Jacinda Ardern, Sanna Marin, Giorgia Meloni, and Mette Frederiksen all came to lead in parliamentary systems. Osmani and Pirc Musar also served as presidents in dual executive systems. Tsai Ing-wen and Maia Sandu rose to power in semi-presidential systems, and Samia Suluhu Hassan and Claudia Sheinbaum ascended through presidential systems.

A country's history also matters. More women leaders have been elected in newer democracies, for instance, including those that emerged from the breakups of the Soviet bloc and Yugoslavia and from Latin America's transition from dictatorship to democracy. Women leaders have also tended to rise at moments of crisis or instability, coming to power on the backs of popular movements against authoritarians or corruption and abuse. Farida Jalazai's large-sample studies have confirmed this pattern, and it has continued to be a factor in recent years.

For example, Tsai, Sandu, Kallas, Mottley, Osmani, and Pirc Musar all ascended to power in periods of crisis. In Taiwan, Tsai's party deliberately sought a woman leader after the country's previous president was tainted by corruption charges; Kallas's party turned to her after its leadership, too, was ensnared in corruption scandals. Sandu emerged at the helm of an anti-corruption protest movement in Moldova that propelled her to power. Pirc Musar was elected president as Slovenians mobilized against Prime Minister Janez Janša's attacks on democratic institutions. Mottley came to power after party leaders tried to oust her and as Barbados teetered on the brink of financial collapse. All these women centered their campaigns on cleaning up corruption, countering injustice, and restoring democracy. Their previous records had established them as defenders of human rights and the rule of law, and their actions and words persuaded voters of their determination and ability to improve government.

These leaders benefited from wide support among youth and women; in all of the countries mentioned, these two groups made up major components of the movements and the grassroots leaders that demanded a change from the status quo. They helped frame demands and enlist wider support. In Slovenia, the youth activist Nika Kovač reached out to pensioners as part of her grassroots democracy campaign that brought the Freedom Movement and Pirc Musar to power. In Taiwan, the Sunflower Student Movement led demands for greater government transparency, a push that also gathered support from older generations. Youth came to represent a key constituency in the growing wave of Taiwanese nationalism. Youth and women also provided important support to Sandu, Kallas, Osmani, and Mottley.

All these women leaders suffered persistent misogynistic attacks during their bids for power but managed to win nonetheless. What made the difference? First, the candidates' increased willingness to call out the sexist attacks was an important development that in turn galvanized public support for them and led to widespread denunciations of the attacks. Tsai confronted sexist attacks directly on the debate stage and on social media. Kallas and Marin were forthright in countering those who had belittled them; countering critics of Marin's viral video, thousands of women posted pictures of themselves dancing to show their support. Students in Kosovo protested and demanded a professor's resignation after he published derogatory comments about Osmani's body and appearance. Sexist defamation that emanated in part from disinformation campaigns, such as those waged by China and Russia in Taiwan, Estonia, and Moldova, was seen and denounced by many as foreign interference.

Organized efforts to document and publicize gendered attacks have also been instrumental in shining a light on the extent of the abuse and the perpetrators. These efforts have exposed the use of artificial means like bots, troll farms, and generative AI to create and propagate falsehoods. Unmasking these tactics makes it harder to deny the attacks and dismiss the violence and sexualized denigration. Some leaders' resilience and reputations have been severely damaged, but many times the public rallies to their defense. In the case of Osmani, she not only won her election despite personal insults against her, but women won a record one-third of parliamentary seats and six of fifteen cabinet posts.

Women have also succeeded by being good coalition builders. Close races in multiparty systems often require the winner to form coalition governments. Kallas initially allied with other parties during her first government, but later her growing popularity propelled her party to an outright majority. In Moldova, deep polarization and relentless attacks from Russia initially forced Sandu to govern with a thin margin, but she later secured outright majorities through exposing her opponents' massive campaign of vote buying and electoral interference. Marin managed a five-party coalition government throughout her tenure; even though all of them were led by women, she engaged in constant negotiations to forge compromises across the spectrum from progressive left to the center. Tsai, for her part, managed multiple challenges to her leadership by striking alliances and outmaneuvering rivals.

As executives in dual power systems, Osmani and Pirc Musar frequently had to manage divergences with their coleaders. Osmani had allied with Prime Minister Albin Kurti in the elections and brought her own stature and popularity to the coalition. When his aggressive moves to shut down illegal Serbian institutions in Kosovo jeopardized U.S. and European support that was essential to any progress the country hoped to make, she used her role as head of state to mitigate friction with Washington and keep the country's quest for full international recognition on track. As Slovenia's head of state, Pirc

Musar sought to play a balancing role as a more centrist president than the left-leaning coalition led by Prime Minister Robert Golob; at times of domestic turmoil, she conveyed the country's abiding commitment as a NATO ally and dependable partner.

GOVERNING RECORDS: DEBUNKING THE STEREOTYPE THAT ONLY MEN CAN LEAD

These women leaders suffered setbacks and committed their share of errors, but their performance shows that they were, on balance, competent leaders who formulated policies and strategies that they executed with fair to high degrees of success. Their record of governance contributes substantially to the evidence that women can indeed govern as capably as men, thus helping to rebut the masculine stereotype that men make better leaders. These women provide powerful role models that should increase public support for future women leaders and encourage more women to enter the political arena.

The women leaders considered in this book displayed strong leadership during their tenures as chief executives, acting decisively and rapidly as needed. They asserted dominance when challenged and did not back down when others sought to overturn their decisions. Such traits form the backbone of the masculine stereotype that men can lead and women cannot. Assertiveness is not the only ingredient of successful leadership, of course. Of equal importance are a propensity to seek information and confer with advisers, experts, and fellow leaders and an ability to negotiate, compromise, and adapt based on results and feedback.

These leaders combined bold decisions with reflection and adaptation in their management styles, sometimes reversing course and at other times holding to their positions when they deemed them vital to the country's interests and needs. For example, Sandu made an early gamble by allying with Igor Dodon to force out Vladimir Plahotniuc. She also took a risk in holding a constitutional referendum to ensure that Moldova's commitment to join the EU would remain even if she were voted out. Tsai took a risk in asserting Taiwan's right to decide its future, knowing that it could trigger a Chinese invasion, but eschewed provocative actions. Pirc Musar and Osmani, both leaders in dual systems, chose to assert their independent powers in foreign affairs, personnel appointments, and constitutional procedures but sought to avoid public spats within the government.

These leaders, to varying degrees, debunked the myth that women cannot conduct national security policy; several of them developed innovative approaches to defending their democracies. Tsai, Sandu, Kallas, Osmani, Marin, and Mottley all formulated security and foreign policy strategies to counter hybrid threats from authoritarian regimes such as China, Russia, and Serbia. Mottley achieved reforms in financial lending practices to enable Barbados and other developing countries to reduce debt and build more resilient economies. Women leaders across the ideological spectrum championed the need to confront authoritarian aggression with sophisticated strategies that went beyond conventional military deterrence. They enacted policies and laws to respond to political, economic, cyber, and informational attacks and shore up their countries' internal weaknesses, including corruption, poverty, political polarization, and energy dependence. The leaders also strengthened their societies by measures to address political and ethnic divisions and improve social and economic well-being.

A major feature of their foreign policies included shoring up alliances and cultivating international support. International diplomacy is vital to the very survival of small countries, which cannot hope to defeat aggressors without outside support. International assistance is also vital to reform their economies and governments and prevent electoral interference, disinformation, and cyberattacks that are waged on an international scale. As Europe came under attack, the EU, NATO, and other bodies became essential elements of the defensive strategy: Kallas, Frederiksen, and Marin were at the forefront of crafting new, stronger alliance policies. In Sandu's case, she knew that Moldova's future stability and security depended on its rapid accession to the EU and secured visible, constant support from France, Germany, and the UK. Pirc Musar used Slovenia's membership in the EU and NATO to repeatedly draw attention to the destabilization of the Western Balkans and advocate for the faster integration of nonmember Balkans states into the EU. Tsai sought to bolster Taiwan's economic and defense relationships, as the country could not hold off Chinese aggression without continued assistance from the United States and other trading partners around the world. NATO responded with its first-ever China strategy and increased exercises in the Indo-Pacific region to deter China's encroachment and violation of international norms.

In domestic policy, many of the women leaders sought to reduce political polarization, reform social welfare programs, and rein in social media and media attacks. They sought to boost growth through expanding trade and economic integration, improving education, and attracting new investment and industries. They also championed climate adaptation and energy resilience as both an economic and a national security imperative.

Gender equality was also an integral part of their domestic and foreign policies. All of the leaders not only stood up against sexism; they actively promoted gender equality reforms and measures to counter hate speech and disinformation. They did so in addition to other social justice efforts, such as Tsai's elevation of Taiwan's multiple indigenous and minority populations and Sandu's outreach to Russian-speaking minorities in Moldova's Transnistria and Gagauzia regions. The leaders passed laws permitting same-sex marriage and protecting against discrimination and sexual harassment in education, government, and the workplace. Most of them achieved gender balance in their cabinets and parties and mentored aspiring women leaders. They sought to convey the message that greater gender equality made for stronger democracy through public forums, podcasts, and speeches as well as women, peace, and security programs to increase women's roles as decision-makers, peacekeepers, security forces, and peace negotiators.

The way the leaders pursued gender equality helped reduce the degree of backlash that such efforts had provoked in the past. They promoted gender equality as an essential feature of democracy but not as an exclusive priority, simultaneously pursuing reforms to benefit the entire society, such as pension, labor, and education reforms. The message was that aspiring to gender equality was not a zero-sum endeavor but one that benefits the entire country. This approach is essential to counter rising discontent among young men. Tsai and other leaders also leaned heavily on the support of younger constituents to pass gender equality reforms and help change views fixed among older generations.

These leaders were not without their failures or shortcomings. All of the leaders lost elections, especially early in their careers. They gradually learned to campaign, to legislate, and to speak in public—in the cases of Tsai and Sandu, overcoming their introversion to do so. Sandu was criticized for being too unyielding, though she was perhaps rightly mistrustful of parties that pretended to support EU integration while receiving support from Russia. Mia Mottley's long dominance in Barbadian politics prompted criticism, as did her frequent travels abroad and the impact of budget cuts. In return, she proposed term limits, but her party declined to adopt them, instead indicating it would continue to support her leadership.

Criticism is not the same thing as failure. Some policies fail; others may have negative consequences but produce net benefits over time. Many of these leaders opted to stick with their policies because they believed they would benefit the majority and serve their countries' long-term interests. Ardern, for example, continued to defend her pandemic-era quarantine and vaccine mandates even though they were perceived to be a main factor in her party's electoral loss. Nonetheless, upon the concurrent releases in June 2025 of her memoir and a documentary film about her time in power, Ardern polled as the most popular politician in New Zealand, which shows how popular judgments of leaders can change over time. Sanna Marin accomplished most of her governing program, but her coalition lost the election because of changing economic and political conditions. Those who stick to their guns may lose elections but turn out to be right in historians' assessments. The willingness to take a stand and be judged by voters is the essence of the political game.

In summary, there is ample evidence that these leaders' governing records were on balance successful. Their policy results demonstrate that they defended their countries from authoritarian attacks, shored up their democracies, and promoted the rights of women and minorities. This success was also demonstrated at the ballot box, as many of the leaders won reelection, some in landslides, and carried their parties to majorities in parliament. These victories reflect the public's approval of their leadership, even if voters disputed specific policies. Many women leaders also had coattail effects, bringing record numbers of women into parliaments and local governments during and after their terms. Mottley, for instance, not only won landslide victories twice but swept every seat in parliament, where women's representation almost doubled. During Ardern's tenure, women exceeded parity in parliament for the first time, a level of representation that fell after her departure. Tsai won landslide elections with legislative majorities, and the number of women in parliament rose during and after her tenure. Most of these leaders also continued to exert influence after they left office, through teaching, speaking, and writing as well as advisory and policy roles on the international stage.

GOING FORWARD: WHAT HELPS WOMEN LEADERS AND DEMOCRACY

How can women build on these records of success going forward? The dire times require a focused approach to achieve rapid success. First, women can rally others to push back on the wholesale war on women that is accelerating with a ferocity not seen in decades. Second, women can play larger roles in the campaign to require safer digital technologies that do not propagate the bigotry, defamation, and disinformation that is poisoning our societies. Third, defense of democracy requires a big-tent effort to strengthen democratic norms, electoral systems, and the rule of law. Women are both vital changemakers and primary beneficiaries in these wider social efforts.

The #MeToo movement broke a code of silence that protected male predators in the entertainment industry and in politics, but the exposure of still prevalent abuse and violence must become a permanent and ongoing practice to delegitimize violence against women. Women are natural leaders in this campaign, but men are indispensable allies and also have a direct stake as fathers, brothers, and sons. Documentation and litigation are important parts of this effort, and in many countries stronger laws are needed. The quest for gender equality has also been set back by massive cuts to foreign assistance, including a dramatic reduction in reproductive and maternal health programs and the gutting of diplomatic and development institutions. A study published in the *Lancet* estimated that American aid cuts could cause some fourteen million deaths by 2030, with knock-on effects for societies and the global economy. For good reason, Hillary Clinton made the global benefits of gender equality a centerpiece of her foreign policy as U.S. secretary of state, and the connections need to be made evident for a new generation of politicians.[2]

Women can also play a leading role in de-escalating the culture war over gender equality. Finding common ground is critical if individuals and families want to return to a place where they can navigate decisions with the help of their communities, doctors, and religious counselors and reaffirm the role that privacy and individual rights used to play in conservative politics and policy. Women can be a major force in fostering the spirit of tolerance and compromise that historically has undergirded successful democracies. Feminists can lay aside rigid litmus tests and look to build a bigger tent of comity. Conservative political leaders can accept the outcomes of the kinds of democratic processes that have legalized abortion in most countries of the world while maintaining their own personal views. Many of the women leaders discussed in this book have promoted gender equality in tandem with other common goals—a deliberate strategy to avoid a zero-sum environment that creates bitterness and gridlock.

A second major challenge that women can play larger roles in addressing is the campaign for safer technology. Given the power and ubiquity of technology in daily life, a wider and more powerful coalition is needed to address significant safety gaps in digital technologies. Artificial intelligence is creating new forms of sexualized violence and distortion, and public understanding of the technologies' impact lags their rapid evolution. Scientists who helped developed AI have warned of catastrophic risks. Geoffrey Hinton, considered the "godfather of AI," quit his position at Google over the company's failure to heed his concerns. He and other experts argue that a "safety by design" approach is more effective than trying to regulate the harms of powerful technologies after they are released. Europol has warned that an explosion of synthetic media could create an "information apocalypse" in which truth and falsehood cannot be distinguished.[1]

Australia and the EU have led in passing laws that require tech companies to enact safety measures. The argument for regulating digital technology rests on the well-established principle that companies are responsible for the safety of their products—a standard that is widely applied to manufacturers of pharmaceuticals and food, for instance. Australia's online safety law, passed in 2015, initially aimed at curbing child pornography. The law was expanded after the 2019 Christchurch massacre to apply to adult users and a wide array of platforms. Julie Inman Grant, the commissioner of the country's eSafety regulatory agency, reports that most tech companies cooperate with the government to address most user complaints, but she has also faced legal challenges from X as well as defamatory statements and death threats targeting her and her family. Australia has also been the pioneer in legislating age restrictions for access to major social media platforms.

Implementation of the EU's tech legislation, specifically the Digital Services Act and AI Act, is a critical test case given that its purview covers the world's third-largest market. The Trump administration threatened punitive tariffs if the EU proceeded to fine U.S. companies for noncompliance, but EU President Ursula von der Leyen insisted that the body would hold fast in implementing the laws. To be successful, campaigns for public policy reform must consider the power of global technology companies and seek allies among them. As a former member of the European Parliament, Marietje Schaake, points out in her 2024 book *The Tech Coup: How to Save Democracy from Silicon Valley*, the market capitalizations of large tech companies exceed the GDPs of most of the world's countries. Some companies have been more sensitive than others to public concerns; for example, Microsoft has been a leader in supporting implementation of the DSA.

While the Trump administration has adopted a generally hostile approach to tech regulation, Congress passed the Take It Down Act in 2025, showing Republican support for some safety measures. The law criminalizes nonconsensual intimate image sharing and requires tech companies to remove the material within forty-eight hours of notice. Because the largest and most powerful tech companies are domiciled in the United States, the single most effective method to incentivize them to pursue effective digital safety measures would be to remove a waiver in Section 230 of the 1996 U.S. Communications Decency Act that shields these companies from liability for harms caused by their products and services.

The third and biggest arena for women's activism is in the defense of democracy. Many women political leaders have been heavily invested, but they can contribute even more by pursuing renewed recruitment efforts and legislating political reforms that make systems more representative. More women candidates are needed to reverse the alarming stall in representation; the attacks on women may spur women to enter politics, as occurred in 2018 in the United States after President Trump's first election. Globally, more women leaders are also needed in top jobs in parties and parliaments. Electoral reforms, such as multimember districts with proportional representation and ranked choice voting, provide for a wider spectrum of political views and representation. The U.S system of single-member districts and winner-take-all voting, together with gerrymandering, fosters the kind of partisan minority dominance so common today. In their 2023 book *Tyranny of the Minority*, the political scientists Steven Levitsky and Daniel Ziblatt list fifteen reforms that could make the U.S. system more representative and thus more democratic. A majority of people around the world prefer democracy over any other system of government, but many are disappointed in the results that democratic governments are delivering. It would be a pyrrhic victory for women to gain fairer political representation only to find their democracies discredited and divided.

A GLOBAL ALLIANCE FOR DEMOCRACY

The trajectory of U.S. democracy is not only a concern for those living in the United States; the effects of its policies, actions, and examples reverberate around the world simply by dint of the country's wealth, military power, and influence. Under the Trump administration, the United States has adopted a transactional approach to international affairs and has retreated from both promoting democracy and adhering to liberal democratic norms. Many countries have reversed their episodes of democratic backsliding, and the United States may prove able to do so as well. In the meantime, however, much progress in defending democracy will depend on other countries.

Women leaders around the world can join with democracy activists and leaders in a global effort to shore up democracy in their countries, their regions, and internationally. More than half of the women leaders currently are in Europe; the continent has distinguished itself both for its stable democracies and for the level of women's representation in them. This critical mass of women leaders has begun to exercise substantial influence and can do more to support women and democracy regionally and internationally. Even though some European countries are experiencing rising right-wing populism or democratic backsliding, the EU has a widely supported and firm architecture of democratic laws and norms to which its twenty-seven member states are bound. The example of its ability to restrain democratic backsliding will be instructive for other regions.

In 2024, the EU reelected Ursula von der Leyen, the first woman European Commission president, to a second term. Roberta Metsola was also reelected to a second term at the helm of the European Parliament. The European Commission elected women to 40 percent of its leadership positions—including Kallas as its foreign affairs and security chief—although it fell short of the parity that von der Leyen had sought. Beyond the EU leadership, the growing tableau of thirteen leaders includes Frederiksen, now serving her second term as Danish prime minister, as well as women leading Iceland, Italy, Kosovo, Latvia, Moldova, North Macedonia, Slovenia, and Ukraine. The Baltic states now rival the Nordic states in normalizing women as prime ministers, speakers of parliament, and heads of the "power ministries": defense, foreign affairs, interior, and finance. Not only are women leaders of these small countries examples at home, but they have equal votes in the EU. The EU's consensus decision-making process helps counterbalance larger countries' greater economic and military weight and gives them equal voice in political decision-making.

Other women leaders have raised their voices for reform of the global governance system to create more equality in decision-making. Women leading international organizations have sought to democratize their bodies and the processes they oversee. Women leaders in Europe form a nucleus of pro-democracy leadership, but they are actively connecting with women leading elsewhere via formal international organizations and groups like Women Political Leaders, the Munich Security Conference, the Reykjavik Global Forum, and Women Deliver. They have been actively engaged in elevating concerns about conflicts, famine, and other crises around the world.

For leaders like Tsai, Russia's war in Ukraine was not a European event but one with direct relevance for China's adventurism in Asia and globally. It reinforced the need to form a global network to push back against authoritarian aggression and repression everywhere. As the United States stepped back from the defense of democracy, many women leaders on the right, left, and center stepped forward to fill the void. The progressive Marin called on Europe to pool its wealth and create a fund of tens of billions of dollars to build a credible deterrent of its own. Frederiksen, a centrist social democrat, urged her counterparts to "remove all self-imposed red lines" to help Ukraine defeat Russia. After Trump berated Zelensky in the Oval Office in February 2025, the center-right Kallas declared, "Today, it became clear that the free world needs a new leader. It is up to us, Europeans, to take this challenge."

The critical mass of women leading in Europe can be a model and source of concrete support for other women around the world, but global problems require new leadership everywhere. The ferment is clear. Coupled with growing frustration with poor governance around the world, a new surge of activism is driving youth to make their voices heard, as they have done in Bangladesh, Nepal, Madagascar, Peru, and elsewhere. Women have stepped forward to lead democracy movements in Belarus, Georgia, and Russia. Supporting and empowering the next generation of leaders, including women, will be critical for the defense of democracy to succeed.

ACKNOWLEDGMENTS

WHEN I BEGAN MY CAREER as a journalist covering Latin America, the region's transition from dictatorship to democracy taught me many lessons. From Chile to Central America and Mexico, I met students, campesinos, and indigenous people, some of whom walked through mountains for days to be able to vote for the first time in their lives, determined to change their government's course. That they succeeded in so many cases convinced me of the power of popular mobilization and the persistent desire for better governance. The many women journalists covering a turbulent region were also an inspiration to me, dogged and intrepid professionals who matched the men story for story. In the following years, as I traveled the world, I met many women change-makers who were instrumental in their countries' paths, even though they were under-recognized and underrepresented in the circles of power. They were unseen in many cases because their stories had never been told.

The themes of how democracies are built and whether they endure have been a through line in my career, not only in Latin America but as a pivotal issue underlying military efforts to achieve security and stability during the two decades of war that followed the 9/11 attacks. I reached sobering conclusions about democracy promotion as the United States strove to engineer it in the difficult conditions of Afghanistan and Iraq. While external support to those struggling for democracy is critical, building a democratic culture and institutions is a generational project that must be driven by change agents in those societies. We are now faced with a global democratic decline that has reached a tipping point with the crisis of democracy in the United States. Here and abroad, women with their numerical power can provide a critical mass in its rebuilding with their energy, talent, and leadership. My mother was an inspiration in her determination and civic engagement even as she battled terminal illness, championing campaign finance and gerrymandering reforms.

Early ideas for this book were germinated in lengthy conversations with Ambassador Nancy McEldowney and Michèle Flournoy shortly after I returned to the Council on Foreign Relations in 2022 as a senior fellow in the Women and Foreign Policy (WFP) program. These two brilliant and accomplished women helped focus my thoughts with their insights and personal experiences from government careers in heavily male environments. Both women have served with great distinction at the highest levels of our foreign policy and national security establishment, and the United States is much the better for it. They are two shining examples among many of women whose acumen in foreign policy and international security match that of any male.

In the ensuing three years of research for this book, I benefited enormously from additional conversations, interviews, and roundtables I convened at the Women and Foreign Policy program with leaders, scholars, practitioners, and activists who have lived and studied the experiences of women political leaders. Sandra Pepera, former director of the Women, Gender, and Democracy program at the National Democratic Institute; Laura Liswood, founder of the Council of Women World Leaders; and Melanne Verveer, the first U.S. ambassador of Global Women's Issues were highly supportive of my quest and generous with their insights. Geeta Rao Gupta, the Biden administration's ambassador for Global Women's Issues, called attention to the nexus of democratic regression and rising headwinds for women leaders with fierce commitment and intellectual focus. The pathbreaking scholarship of Valerie Hudson, Farida Jalalzai, and Mona Lena Krook on women and politics provided an essential foundation for my effort to understand the current moment for women political leaders at the national executive level.

I am grateful to Jim Lindsay and Richard Haass for inviting me back to the Council on Foreign Relations, and to Mike Froman, the president of the Council. My early career start at *Foreign Affairs* magazine and mentorship by editors Bill Hyland and James Chace were invaluable, as was the support of Ambassador George Landau, who headed the CFR Task

Force on Central America and commissioned me to write *Intervention or Neglect*, my first book, about U.S. policy and the Central American peace process. In my latest return to the Council, Shannon O'Neil has provided welcome support and guidance as the senior vice president and director of studies; both she and her deputy, Senior Fellow Stuart Reid, provided incisive reviews that greatly improved this book. My colleagues Senior Fellow Joshua Kurlantzick and Research Fellow Jacob Ware contributed detailed notes on many chapters that illuminated gaps, challenged my thinking, and imparted their considerable expertise on democracy and extremism. Many other CFR colleagues provided illuminating comments about their areas and regions of expertise, including Will Freeman, Kat Duffy, David Sacks, Michelle Gavin, Ebenezer Obadare, Liana Fox, David Scheffer, and Rebecca Lissner. The Fellows Virtual Brown Bag group led by Sheila Smith and Sebastian Mallaby helped me clarify and sharpen my arguments. Few organizations can boast such a wealth of diverse expertise in a collegial environment. CFR managing director of publications Trish Dorff supported me throughout the publication process. Special thanks are due to my gifted and tirelessly cheerful research associate, Noël Sedona James, who contributed to every facet of this project and supplied many helpful comments. WFP program interns Egunyale (Naimah) Haynes, Imaan Mirza, and Uma Fox also provided invaluable research assistance under Noël's guidance.

Caelyn Cobb, senior editor for global history and politics at Columbia University Press, welcomed this project and provided expert guidance throughout the process. I thank her, assistant editor Alex Gupta, production editor Kat Jorge, copy-editor Peggy Tropp, and the entire team at Columbia University Press, along with the two expert peer reviewers CUP commissioned, for their critiques, suggestions, and skill in shepherding the book into its final form. Kate Brannen helped me think through early drafts of the first chapters. Neither this book, nor any of my previous books, would exist without the wisdom, support, and friendship of the indomitable Flip Brophy, my agent and president of Sterling Lord Literistic. I'm indebted as well to SLL agent Jessica Friedman for her help. Other friends and most of all my husband Scott—always my first reader—gave generously of their time and love. Compensation in deckhand duty is forthcoming. All errors are my own.

NOTES

INTRODUCTION

1. EIU Democracy Index, "EIU's 2024 Democracy Index: Trend of Global Democratic Decline and Strengthening Authoritarianism Continues Through 2024," February 27, 2025, Economist Intelligence Unit, https://www.eiu.com/n/democracy-index-2024/.

2. Erica Chenoweth and Zoe Marks, "Revenge of the Patriarchs: Why Autocrats Fear Women," *Foreign Affairs* 101, no. 2 (March/April 2022): 103–116.

3. Valerie Hudson, Donna Lee Bowen, and Perpetua Lynne Nielsen, *The First Political Order: How Sex Shapes Governance and National Security Worldwide* (New York: Columbia University Press, 2020).

4. Helle Thorning-Schmidt, speaking on "The Outlook for Women's Political Leadership in 2024," Council on Foreign Relations, March 8, 2024, https://www.cfr.org/event/outlook-womens-political-leadership-2024.

5. Mona Lena Krook, "Violence Against Women in Politics," *Journal of Democracy* 28, no. 1 (2017): 74–88, https://doi.org/10.1353/jod.2017.0007. Krook defined the phenomenon as "(1) aggressive acts aimed largely or solely at women in politics; (2) because they are women, often using gendered means of attack; and (3) with the goal of deterring their

participation in order to preserve traditional gender roles and undermine democratic institutions. It is worth noting that the understanding of 'violence' is not limited to physical manifestations, although words such as 'harassment,' 'intimidation,' 'abuse,' and 'discrimination' may be used in conjunction with 'violence' to draw attention to nonphysical acts of resistance to women's participation. Researchers and activists tend to use 'violence' in this context as an umbrella concept that includes all these things as well as acts of physical coercion."

6. Tatum Hunter, "Trump's 'Grab Them' Comment Was History: Now TikTok Is Showing It to Young Voters," *Washington Post*, October 31, 2024; Sam Meredith, "Who Is the 'Trump of the Tropics?': Brazil's Divisive New President, Jair Bolsonaro—in His Own Words," CNBC, October 29, 2018; "Duterte Jokes About Rape, Again: Philippine Women Aren't Laughing," *New York Times*, August 31, 2018, https://www .nytimes.com/2018/08/31/world/asia/philippines-rodrigo-duterte-rape -joke.html.

7. Ashleigh Fields, "Appeals Court Closes Out Trump's Bid to Overturn Carroll Verdict," *The Hill*, July 10, 2025, https://thehill.com/homenews/ administration/5395961-judges-rule-against-trump-appeal-in-e-jean- carroll-case/.

8. Ashifa Kassam, "Online Vitriol Could Undo Decades of Political Progress, Warns Dutch Deputy PM," *Guardian*, November 3, 2023, https:// www.theguardian.com/world/2023/nov/03/online-vitriol-could-undo -decades-political-progress-dutch-deputy-pm.

9. Danielle Gianmarco, "Why Are Female Politicians More Often Targeted with Violence? New Findings Confirm Depressing Suspicions," *Conversation*, November 26, 2024, https://theconversation.com/why-are -female-politicians-more-often-targeted-with-violence-new-findings -confirm-depressing-suspicions-238483.

10. Silvana Koch-Mehrin, speaking on "The Outlook for Women's Political Leadership in 2024," Council on Foreign Relations, March 8, 2024, https://www.cfr.org/event/outlook-womens-political-leadership-2024.

11. Krook, "Violence Against Women in Politics."

12. Vibeke Venema, Stephanie Hegarty, and Leoni Robertson, "Growth of Women in Power Grinds to Near-Halt in a Mega-Election Year," BBC News, December 28, 2024, https://www.bbc.com/news/articles/cy8951 25gwxo. Data on U.S. Congress is from Kelly Ditmar, *Women in Election 2024: Stalled Progress*, Center for American Women and Politics,

Eagleton Institute of Politics, Rutgers University, 2025, https://women run.rutgers.edu/2024-report/congress/.

13. Council on Foreign Relations, "Women's Power Index," updated August 7, 2025, https://www.cfr.org/article/womens-power-index. The database excludes monarchs and includes women who are democratically selected with individual authority as heads of state and government of UN member states. Detailed criteria are listed at the site's methodology tab.

14. Our World in Data, "Women's Political Participation Index, 2024: Key Features of Women's Political Empowerment, World," https://ourworld indata.org/grapher/women-political-participation-index.

15. Jon Levine, "Trump Says If Kamala Harris Wins US 'Three Days Away' from Depression: 'Joe Biden Is Herbert Hoover,'" *New York Post*, November 2, 2024, https://nypost.com/2024/11/02/us-news/trump-warns-of -depression-in-kamala-harris-wins/.

16. Isaac Arnsdorf, "Trump Suggests Harris Would Struggle with World Leaders Based on Her Appearance," *Washington Post*, August 2, 2024, https://www.washingtonpost.com/politics/2024/07/30/trump-harris -play-toy-comment/.

17. Linda Robinson and Noël James, "Women's Power Index," Council on Foreign Relations, updated August 7, 2025, https://www.cfr.org/tracker /womens-power-index#chapter-title-0-4; Pedro Conceição et al., *2023 Gender Social Norms Index* (New York: United Nations Development Programme, 2023), https://hdr.undp.org/system/files/documents/hdp -document/gsni202303.pdf, 12.

1. THE TANDEM CRISIS OF DEMOCRACY
AND WOMEN'S LEADERSHIP

The epigraph is taken from "A Clarion Call for Gender Equality: Secretary-General's Remarks at the Opening of the 69th Session of the Commission on the Status of Women," United Nations Sustainable Development Group, March 10, 2025, https://unsdg.un.org/latest/announcements /clarion-call-gender-equality-secretary-generals-remarks-opening-69th -session.

1. Some material in this chapter was previously published in Linda Robinson, "The Global Assault on Women in Politics," *Foreign Affairs*, July 3, 2024, https://www.foreignaffairs.com/world/global-assault-women-pol itics-linda-robinson.

2. Yana Gorokhovskaia and Cathryn Grothe, *Freedom in the World: The Uphill Battle to Safeguard Rights* (Washington, DC: Freedom House, 2025), https://freedomhouse.org/report/freedom-world/2025/uphill-battle-to-safeguard-rights.

3. These studies were based on surveys of seventy and 173 countries, respectively. Christian Welzel, Pippa Norris, and Ronald Inglehart, "Gender Equality and Democracy," *Comparative Sociology* 1, no. 3–4 (2002): 321–345, https://doi.org/10.1163/156913302100418628; Yi-Ting Wang et al., "Women's Rights in Democratic Transitions: A Global Sequence Analysis, 1900–2012," *European Journal of Political Research* 56, no. 4 (2017): 735–756, https://doi.org/10.1111/1475-6765.12201.

4. Ted Piccone, "Democracy and Security Dialogue Policy Brief Series: Democracy, Gender Equality, and Security," Brookings Institution, September 2017, https://www.brookings.edu/articles/democracy-gender-equality-and-security/.

5. Elena Ortiz et al., *Exploring the Links Between Women's Status and Democracy* (Washington, DC: Georgetown Institute for Women, Peace and Security, 2023). The study determined correlation coefficients for free elections (.74), free association and assembly (.63), and checks on executive power (.67) among the ninety-six countries Freedom House rated as either free or partly free.

6. United Nations, "Report of the World Conference of the International Women's Year: Mexico City 19 June–2 July 1975," 1976, https://docs.un.org/en/E/CONF.66/34, 132.

7. Inter-Parliamentary Union, "Women in Parliament 1995–2025," 2025, https://www.ipu.org/resources/publications/reports/2025-03/women-in-parliament-1995-2025, 3; Inter-Parliamentary Union, "Women in Politics: 2025," 2025, https://www.ipu.org/resources/publications/infographics/2025-03/women-in-politics-2025.

8. Vibeke Venema, Stephanie Hegarty, and Leoni Robertson, "Growth of Women in Power Grinds to Near-Halt in a Mega-Election Year," BBC News, December 28, 2024, https://www.bbc.com/news/articles/cy895l25gwxo; Center for American Women and Politics, "Women in the 119th Congress," press release, January 2, 2025, https://cawp.rutgers.edu/news-media/press-releases/women-119th-congress.

9. Kusum Kali Pal et al., *Global Gender Gap 2024: Insight Report*, World Economic Forum, June 11, 2024, 13, 18.

10. Brian F. Schaffner, Matthew Macwilliams, and Tatishe Nteta, "Understanding White Polarization in the 2016 Vote for President: The Sobering Role of Racism and Sexism," *Political Science Quarterly* 133, no. 1 (2018): 9–34, https://doi.org/10.1002/polq.12737.

11. Daren E. J. Austin and Mervyn Jackson, "Benevolent and Hostile Sexism Differentially Predicted by Facets of Right-Wing Authoritarianism and Social Dominance Orientation," *Personality and Individual Differences* 139 (2019): 34–38, https://doi.org/10.1016/j.paid.2018.11.002; Orly Bareket and Susan T. Fiske, "A Systematic Review of the Ambivalent Sexism Literature: Hostile Sexism Protects Men's Power; Benevolent Sexism Guards Traditional Gender Roles," *Psychological Bulletin* 149, no. 11–12 (2023): 637–698, https://doi.org/10.1037/bul0000400.

12. Nicholas A. Valentino, Carly Wayne, and Marzia Oceno, "Mobilizing Sexism: The Interaction of Emotion and Gender Attitudes in the 2016 US Presidential Election," *Public Opinion Quarterly* 82, no. S1 (2018): 799–821, https://doi.org/10.1093/poq/nfy003.

13. Susanne Reinhardt, Annett Heft, and Elena Pavan, "Varieties of Anti-genderism: The Politicization of Gender Issues Across Three European Populist Radical Right Parties," *Information, Communication & Society* 27, no. 7 (2023): 1273–1294, https://doi.org/10.1080/1369118X.2023.2246536.

14. Ipsos and Global Institute for Women's Leadership at King's College London, *International Women's Day 2024 Report*, March 2024, https://www.ipsos.com/en-us/millennials-and-gen-z-less-favour-gender-equality-older-generations.

15. This book is focused on women in all their diversity and recognizes the overlap in many cases with a range of LGBTQ issues. It also recognizes that women of color and marginalized communities are disproportionately affected. For brevity, women will be understood to refer to all women.

16. Teri Schultz, "Why Trump Is Lavishing Praise on Hungarian Prime Minister Viktor Orban," *Morning Edition*, NPR, August 20, 2024, https://www.npr.org/2024/08/20/nx-s1-5075164/why-trump-is-lavishing-praise-on-hungarian-prime-minister-viktor-orban.

17. Jeremy Shapiro and Zsuzsanna Végh, "The Orbanisation of America: Hungary's Lessons for Donald Trump," European Council on Foreign Relations, October 9, 2024, https://ecfr.eu/publication/the-orbanisation-of-america-hungarys-lessons-for-donald-trump/.

18. Johann Sonnenburg, "Political Mobilization in Germany," V-Dem Institute, February 20, 2025, https://www.v-dem.net/gow.html.

19. Felix Schlagwein, "Viktor Orbán's War on LGBT+ People in Hungary," *Deutsche Welle*, May 21, 2020, https://www.dw.com/en/viktor-orban-expands-hungarys-anti-lgbtq-measures/a-53526969; Maya Oppenheim, "Hungarian Prime Minister Viktor Orban Bans Gender Studies Programmes," *Independent*, October 25, 2018, https://www.independent.co.uk/news/world/europe/hungary-bans-gender-studies-programmes-viktor-orban-central-european-university-budapest-a8599796.html; Balázs Pivarnyik, "Family and Gender in Orbán's Hungary," Heinrich Böll Foundation, July 4, 2018, https://www.boell.de/en/2018/07/04/family-and-gender-viktor-orbans-hungary.

20. Andrea Krizsán and Conny Roggeband, *Politicizing Gender and Democracy in the Context of the Istanbul Convention* (Cham: Palgrave Macmillan, 2021).

21. Maïa de La Baume, "How the Istanbul Convention Became a Symbol of Europe's Cultural Wars," *Politico*, April 12, 2021, https://www.politico.eu/article/istanbul-convention-europe-violence-against-women/.

22. Sara Kalm and Anna Meeuwisse, "Transcalar Activism Contesting the Liberal International Order: The Case of the World Congress of Families," *Social Politics: International Studies in Gender, State & Society* 30, no. 2 (2023): 556–579, https://doi.org/10.1093/sp/jxad001.

23. Agence France-Presse, "Slovakian President Čaputová Says She Will Not Run for Re-election," *Guardian*, June 20, 2023, https://www.theguardian.com/world/2023/jun/20/slovakia-president-zuzana-caputova-says-she-will-not-run-for-re-election.

24. Eva Anduiza and Guillem Rico, "Sexism and the Far-Right Vote: The Individual Dynamics of Gender Backlash," *American Journal of Political Science,* 68, no. 2 (2022): 478–493, https://onlinelibrary.wiley.com/doi/full/10.1111/ajps.12759.

25. European Commission, *The European Union—What It Is and What It Does* (Luxembourg: Publications Office of the European Union, 2022), https://op.europa.eu/webpub/com/eu-what-it-is/en/#chapter2_44.

26. Laura Bicker, "Why Misogyny Is at the Heart of South Korea's Presidential Elections," BBC News, March 7, 2022, https://www.bbc.com/news/world-asia-60643446.

27. Freedom House, *South Korea: Freedom in the World 2024 Country Report*, February 2024, https://freedomhouse.org/country/south-korea/freedom-world/2024.

28. Mark R. Thompson, "Dynasties' Daughters and Martyrs' Widows: Female Leaders and Gender Inequality in Asia," *Disruptive Asia* 5, 2022, https://disruptiveasia.asiasociety.org/dynasties-daughters-and-martyrs -widows-female-leaders-and-gender-inequality-in-asia.

29. "'The Hostility Was Something I'd Never Experienced Before': The Cost to Women of the Overlooked Rise of Kenya's Manosphere," CNN, https://www.cnn.com/interactive/asequals/kenya-manosphere-toxic -masculinity-as-equals/.

30. Obiageli Ezekwesili, interviewed by Linda Robinson, November 2023.

31. Liubov Tsareva, "Fighting the Patriarchy in Mother Russia," *Truthdig*, June 8, 2023, https://www.truthdig.com/articles/fighting-the-patriarchy -in-mother-russia/.

32. Kristina Stoeckl, "The Rise of the Russian Christian Right: The Case of the World Congress of Families," *Religion, State and Society* 48, no. 4 (2020): 223–238, https://doi.org/10.1080/09637494.2020.1796172.

33. Leta Hong Fincher, *Leftover Women: The Resurgence of Gender Inequality in China* (London: Bloomsbury, 2014).

34. The Hindu Bureau, "India 'One of the Worst Autocratisers': V-Dem Report on Democracy," *Hindu*, March 11, 2024, https://www.thehindu .com/news/national/india-one-of-the-worst-autocratisers-v-dem -report-on-democracy/article67939573.ece.

35. Amnesty International, "New Study Shows Shocking Scale of Abuse on Twitter Against Women Politicians in India," press release, January 23, 2020, https://www.amnestyusa.org/press-releases/shocking-scale-of-abuse -on-twitter-against-women-politicians-in-india/.

36. Gretel Kauffman, "US No Longer a 'Full Democracy' in 2016 Democracy Index: Where Do We Go from Here?," *Christian Science Monitor*, https://www.csmonitor.com/USA/2017/0126/US-no-longer-a-full -democracy-in-2016-Democracy-Index-Where-do-we-go-from -here.

37. Nicholas Nehamas and Erica L. Green, "Trump Says He'll Protect Women, 'Like It or Not,' Evoking His History of Misogyny," *New York Times*, October 31, 2024, https://www.nytimes.com/2024/10/31/us/poli tics/trump-women-like-it-or-not.html.

38. Isaac Arnsdorf, "Trump Suggests Harris Would Struggle with World Leaders Based on Her Appearance," *Washington Post,* August 2, 2024, https://www.washingtonpost.com/politics/2024/07/30/trump-harris -play-toy-comment/.

39. Michael Gold, "Trump Reposts Crude Sexual Remark About Harris on Truth Social," *New York Times*, August 28, 2024, updated November 8, 2024, https://www.nytimes.com/2024/08/28/us/politics/trump-truth -social-posts.html.

40. Editorial Board, "Donald Trump's Closing Argument: Vulgarity," *Washington Post*, October 29, 2024, https://www.washingtonpost.com/opin ions/2024/10/29/trump-vulgar-rally-profanity/.

41. Louise K. Davidson-Schmich, Farida Jalalzai, and Malliga Och, "Crisis, Gender Role Congruency, and Perceptions of Executive Leadership," *Politics & Gender* 19, no. 3 (2023): 900–907, https://doi.org/10.1017/S174 3923X22000411.

42. Tess McClure, "New Zealand Anti–Vaccine Mandate Protests: Police and Photographer Attacked," *Guardian*, November 8, 2021, https://www .theguardian.com/world/2021/nov/09/new-zealand-anti-vaccine-man date-protests-police-and-photographer-attacked.

43. Praveen Menon, "New Zealand's Ardern Labels Anti–Vaccine Mandate Protests 'Imported' as Crowds Defy Calls to Leave," Reuters, February 14, 2022, https://www.reuters.com/world/asia-pacific/new-zealands-ard ern-labels-anti-vaccine-mandate-protests-imported-crowds-defy-2022 -02-14/.

44. Byron Clark, "FRONTLINE 3: The NZ Media and the Occupation of Parliament," *Pacific Journalism Review: Te Koakoa* 28 (2022): 123–137, https://doi.org/10.24135/pjr.v28i1and2.1248.

45. Radio New Zealand, "Jacinda Ardern Resigns: Social Media 'Cesspit' Blamed for Growing Threats, Abuse Towards Politicians," RNZ, January 20, 2023, https://www.rnz.co.nz/news/political/482820/jacinda-ardern -resigns-social-media-cesspit-blamed-for-growing-threats-abuse -towards-politicians.

46. Chris Wilson, "How Data Shines a Light on the Online Hatred for Jacinda Ardern," *Stuff*, January 23, 2023, https://www.auckland.ac.nz/en /news/2023/01/24/data-shines-a-light-on-the-online-hatred-for -jacinda-ardern.html.

47. Jacinda Ardern, *A Different Kind of Power: A Memoir* (New York: Crown, 2025).

48. Jackson Katz, "Violence Against Jacinda Ardern and Other Women Political Leaders Is an Attack on Democracy Itself," *Ms.*, January 31, 2023, https://msmagazine.com/2023/01/31/jacinda-ardern-violence-women/.

2. MAINSTREAMING THE FAR RIGHT AND VIOLENT MISOGYNY

1. An exception was this report: Anti-Defamation League, *When Women Are the Enemy: The Intersection of Misogyny and White Supremacy*, July 2018, https://www.adl.org/resources/report/when-women-are-enemy -intersection-misogyny-and-white-supremacy.

2. Alexandra Phelan et al., *Introductory Guide to Understanding Misogyny and the Far Right*, Centre for Research and Evidence on Security Threats, February 20, 2023, https://crestresearch.ac.uk/resources/intro ductory-guide-to-understanding-misogyny-and-the-far-right/.

3. United Nations Development Programme Oslo Governance Centre, *Misogyny: The Extremist Gateway*, June 16, 2021, https://www.undp.org /policy-centre/governance/publications/misogyny-extremist-gateway.

4. Fredrik Wilhelmsen, "'The Wife Would Put on a Nice Suit, Hat, and Possibly Gloves': The Misogynistic Identity Politics of Anders Behring Breivik," *Fascism* 10, no. 1 (2021): 108–133, https://doi.org/10.1163/22116257 -10010003.

5. John Hooper, "Ex-Berlusconi Minister Defends Anders Behring Breivik," *Guardian*, July 27, 2011, https://www.theguardian.com/world /2011/jul/27/ex-berlusconi-minister-defends-breivik.

6. Jacob Davey and Julia Ebner, *'The Great Replacement': The Violent Consequences of Mainstreamed Extremism* (London: Institute for Strategic Dialogue, 2019).

7. Gionathan Lo Mascolo and Kristina Stoeckl, "The Rise of the Christian Right in Europe," Canopy Forum, November 6, 2024, https://canopy forum.org/2024/11/06/the-rise-of-the-christian-right-in-europe/; Camila Vergara, "How Christian Nationalism Is Taking Root Across the World," *Politico*, October 27, 2022, https://www.politico.com/news/magazine /2022/10/27/global-far-right-christian-nationalists-00063400; Dube, Siphiwe, "Christian Nationalism in Post-Apartheid South Africa: From the White Broederbond to the Transracial Neo/Pentecostals," *International Journal for the Study of the Christian Church* 23, no. 4 (2023): 382–406, https://doi.org/10.1080/1474225X.2023.2275839.

8. "Christian Nationalism Across All 50 States: Insights from PRRI's 2024 American Values Atlas," Public Religion Research Institute, February 4, 2025, https://prri.org/research/christian-nationalism-across-all-50-states -insights-from-prris-2024-american-values-atlas/.

9. Liam Adams, "Why Pete Hegseth Nomination Is a Milestone for the Rightwing Christian Movement He Follows," *USA Today*, January 13, 2025, https://www.usatoday.com/story/news/politics/elections/2025/01/13/pete-hegseth-nomination-is-milestone-for-doug-wilsons-church-movement/76947642007/; Jason Wilson, "Revealed: Trump Pentagon Nominee Endorsed Extremist Christian Doctrine on Podcast," *Guardian*, January 24, 2025, https://www.theguardian.com/us-news/2025/jan/24/trump-pete-hegseth-extremism.

10. Julia Simon, "Defense Secretary Pete Hegseth Reposts Video of Pastors Saying Women Shouldn't Vote," NPR, August 9, 2025, https://www.npr.org/2025/08/09/nx-s1-5497226/women-pastor-pete-hegseth-vote.

11. Monica Hesse, "JD Vance's Repeated Digs at Childless Women Are Worse Than You Thought," *Washington Post*, September 4, 2024, https://www.washingtonpost.com/style/power/2024/09/04/jd-vance-women-children/; Sarah Jones, "J.D. Vance and the Rise of the 'Postliberal' Catholics," *New York Magazine*, September 22, 2024, https://nymag.com/intelligencer/article/j-d-vance-and-the-rise-of-the-postliberal-catholics.html; Paul Elie, "J.D. Vance's Radical Religion," *New Yorker*, July 24, 2024, https://www.newyorker.com/news/daily-comment/j-d-vances-radical-religion; Erica Sloan, "Just a List of the Bizarre, Gross, and Upsetting Things JD Vance Has Said About Women," *Self*, October 1, 2024, https://www.self.com/story/jd-vance-views-women.

12. Sara Brzuszkiewicz, "Incel Radical Milieu and External Locus of Control," International Centre for Counter-Terrorism–The Hague, November 25, 2020, https://icct.nl/sites/default/files/import/publication/Special-Edition-2-1.pdf.

13. Lucy Nicholas et al., "Antifeminist, Manosphere, and Right-Wing Extremist Sentiment Among Men Who Use Domestic and Family Violence: Masculinism, Misinformation, and the Justificatory Logics of Violence," *NORMA*, 2024, 1–20, https://doi.org/10.1080/18902138.2024.2430513.

14. Bruce Hoffman and Jacob Ware, "Are We Entering a New Era of Far-Right Terrorism?" War on the Rocks, November 27, 2019, https://warontherocks.com/2019/11/are-we-entering-a-new-era-of-far-right-terrorism/.

15. Craig Haslop et al., "Mainstreaming the Manosphere's Misogyny Through Affective Homosocial Currencies: Exploring How Teen Boys

Navigate the Andrew Tate Effect," *Social Media + Society* 10, no. 1 (2024), doi.org/10.1177/20563051241228811.

16. Josie Ensor, "How Trump Allies Helped Pave the Way for Andrew Tate's Return," *Times*, March 14, 2025, https://www.thetimes.com/us/news -today/article/andrew-tristan-tate-trump-miami-9tnjfvvnx.

17. Katie Herchenroeder, "Emboldened Men Celebrate Donald Trump's Win by Hurling Attacks on Women Online," *Vanity Fair*, November 9, 2024, https://www.vanityfair.com/news/story/donald-trump-nick-fuen tes-your-body-my-choice-4b?srsltid=AfmBOoqTs3eb97jw-7RJQzPgua J3bv_cfvBTJoEGkxoBteQHaosgK-nD.

18. Right Wing Watch (@RightWingWatch), posted a clip of Fuentes saying in his America First streaming show on cozy.tv: "We need to go back to burning women alive more." X, June 2, 2022, 2:39 p.m., https://x .com/rightwingwatch/status/1532431796301971456?lang=en.

19. Mona Krook and Juliana Restrepo, "The Cost of Doing Politics? Analyzing Violence and Harassment Against Female Politicians," *Perspectives on Politics* 18, no. 3 (2020): 740–755, https://doi.org/10.1017/S1537592 719001397.

20. Helen Catt and Charlotte Rose, "Misogyny to Be Treated as Extremism by UK Government," BBC News, August 18, 2024, https://www.bbc .com/news/articles/c15gnolq7p50.

21. Francesca Gillett, "Influencers Driving Extreme Misogyny, Say Police," BBC News, July 22, 2024, https://www.bbc.com/news/articles/cne4 vw1x83po

22. National Police Chiefs' Council, "Call to Action as Violence Against Women and Girls Epidemic Deepens," press release, July 23, 2024, https://news.npcc.police.uk/releases/call-to-action-as-violence-against -women-and-girls-epidemic-deepens-1#:~:text=The%20National%20 Policing%20Statement%20for,37%25%20between%202018%2F23.

23. Arna Carlock and Meagan Cutler, "Mass Attacks in Public Spaces: 2016–2020," (Washington, DC: United States Secret Service, National Threat Assessment Center, 2023), https://www.secretservice.gov/sites /default/files/reports/2023-01/usss-ntac-maps-2016-2020.pdf.

24. Inter-Parliamentary Union, *Sexism, Harassment and Violence Against Women Parliamentarians*, October 2016, https://www.ipu.org/resources /publications/issue-briefs/2016-10/sexism-harassment-and-violence -against-women-parliamentarians.

25. Inter-Parliamentary Union, "Widespread Sexism and Violence Against Women in African Parliaments According to New IPU Report," press release, November 23, 2021, https://www.ipu.org/news/press-releases /2021-11/widespread-sexism-and-violence-against-women-in-african -parliaments-according-new-ipu-report.

26. Inter-Parliamentary Union, *Sexism, Harassment and Violence Against Women in Parliaments in the Asia-Pacific Region*, March 2025, https:// www.ipu.org/resources/publications/issue-briefs/2025-03/sexism-harass ment-and-violence-against-women-in-parliaments-in-asia-pacific -region.

27. Mona Lena Krook, *Violence Against Women in Politics* (Oxford: Oxford University Press, 2020), https://doi.org/10.1093/oso/9780190088460.001 .0001.

28. Roudabeh Kishi, "Violence Targeting Women in Politics," The Armed Conflict Location & Event Data Project (ACLED), December 2021, https://acleddata.com/sites/default/files/wp-content-archive/uploads /2021/12/ACLED_Report_PVTWIP_2021.pdf.

29. Maggie Astor, "For Female Candidates, Harassment and Threats Come Every Day," *New York Times*, August 24, 2018, https://www.nytimes.com /2018/08/24/us/politics/women-harassment-elections.html.

30. Dareh Gregorian and Zoë Richards, "Virginia Man Charged with Threatening to Kill Kamala Harris," NBC News, August 5, 2024, https:// www.nbcnews.com/politics/politics-news/virginia-man-charged-threat ening-kill-kamala-harris-rcna165280.

31. Stephanie Lai, Luke Broadwater, and Carl Hulse, "Lawmakers Confront a Rise in Threats and Intimidation, and Fear Worse," *New York Times*, October 1, 2022, https://www.nytimes.com/2022/10/01/us/politics /violent-threats-lawmakers.html.

32. Michael Gold, "Trump, Vance, and Allies Hurl Insults at Women as Race Ends," *New York Times*, https://www.nytimes.com/2024/11/05/us /politics/trump-nancy-pelosi-liz-cheney-women.html.

33. Karlijn Saris and Coen van de Ven, "Misogyny as a Political Weapon," *De Groene Amsterdammer*, March 3, 2021, https://www.groene.nl/artikel /misogynie-als-politiek-wapen.

34. "Conspiracy Theorist Visit Was 'Absurd and Frightening,' Says Kaag," *DutchNews.nl*, January 6, 2022, https://www.dutchnews.nl/2022/01/cons piracy-theorist-visit-was-absurd-and-frightening-says-kaag/.

3. TECHNOLOGY'S DISPROPORTIONATE TOLL
ON WOMEN POLITICIANS

1. Kristina Van Sant, Rolf Fredheim, and Gundars Bergmanis-Korāts, *Abuses of Power: Coordinated Online Harassment of Finnish Government Ministers* (Riga: NATO Strategic Communications Centre of Excellence, 2021), https://stratcomcoe.org/publications/abuse-of-power-coor dinated-online-harassment-of-finnish-government-ministers/5.

2. Leonie Cater, "Finland's Women-Led Government Targeted by Online Harassment," *Politico*, March 17, 2021, https://www.politico.eu /article/sanna-marin-finland online-harassment-women-government -targeted/.

3. RFE/RL, "Finnish Support for NATO Membership Rises to 78 Percent, Poll Shows," Radio Free Europe/Radio Liberty, November 23, 2022, https://www.rferl.org/a/finland-nato-survey-membership/32145117 .html.

4. Imogen West-Knights, "Three Women Leading Their Countries Quit Using Strikingly Similar Language: Does It Tell Us Anything?" *Slate*, April 5, 2023, https://slate.com/news-and-politics/2023/04/sanna-marin -finland-election-jacinda-ardern-nicola-sturgeon.html.

5. Essi Lehto, "Finland's Marin, Once the World's Youngest Premier, Steps Down as Party Leader," Reuters, September 1, 2023, https://www .reuters.com/world/europe/finlands-marin-once-worlds-youngest-pre mier-steps-down-party-leader-2023-09-01/.

6. Kayla Webley Adler, "Sanna Marin Is Still Dancing," *Elle*, January 25, 2024, https://www.elle.com/culture/career-politics/a46271349/sanna-marin -interview-2024/.

7. Inter-Parliamentary Union, *Sexism, Harassment and Violence Against Women Parliamentarians*, October 2016, https://www.ipu.org/resources /publications/issue-briefs/2016-10/sexism-harassment-and-violence -against-women-parliamentarians.

8. Inter-Parliamentary Union and Assembly of the Council of Europe, *Sexism, Harassment and Violence Against Women in Europe*, October 2018, https://www.ipu.org/resources/publications/issue-briefs/2018-10/sexism -harassment-and-violence-against-women-in-parliaments-in-europe; Inter-Parliamentary Union and African Parliamentary Union, *Sexism, Harassment and Violence Against Women in Africa*, November 2021, https://

www.ipu.org/resources/publications/issue-briefs/2021-11/sexism-harassment-and-violence-against-women-in-parliaments-in-africa.

9. The Economist Intelligence Unit, *Measuring the Prevalence of Online Violence Against Women*, March 1, 2021, https://onlineviolencewomen.eiu.com/.

10. Elle Hunt, Nick Evershed, and Ri Liu, "From Julia Gillard to Hillary Clinton: Online Abuse of Politicians Around the World," *Guardian*, June 26, 2016, https://www.theguardian.com/technology/datablog/ng-interactive/2016/jun/27/from-julia-gillard-to-hillary-clinton-online-abuse-of-politicians-around-the-world.

11. Dhanaraj Thakur, "Women of Color Political Candidates in the US Endure Most Severe Online Abuse, Mis- and Disinformation," Center for Democracy and Technology, October 27, 2022, https://cdt.org/insights/women-of-color-political-candidates-in-the-us-endure-most-severe-online-abuse-mis-and-disinformation/.

12. Dhanaraj Thakur and Müge Finkel, "Hated More: Online Violence Targeting Women of Color Candidates in the 2024 US Election," Center for Democracy & Technology, October 2, 2024, https://cdt.org/insights/report-hated-more-online-violence-targeting-women-of-color-candidates-in-the-2024-us-election/.

13. Frances Perraudin and Simon Murphy, "Alarm Over Number of Female MPs Stepping Down After Abuse," *Guardian*, October 31, 2019, https://www.theguardian.com/politics/2019/oct/31/alarm-over-number-female-mps-stepping-down-after-abuse.

14. Sean Coughlan, "Theresa May Attacks 'Vile' Online Threats Against Women," BBC News, June 7, 2018, https://www.bbc.com/news/education-44402658.

15. Sharon Goulds, *State of the World's Girls 2021: The Truth Gap* (Woking: Plan International, 2021), https://plan-international.org/uploads/2022/02/sotwgr2021-commsreport-en.pdf.

16. #ShePersisted, "Our Work," 2024, https://she-persisted.org/our-work/research-and-thought-leadership/; Lucina Di Meco, *Monetizing Misogyny: Gendered Disinformation and the Undermining of Women's Rights and Democracy Globally* (#ShePersisted, February 2023), https://she-persisted.org/wp-content/uploads/2023/02/ShePersisted_MonetizingMisogyny.pdf.

17. Irene Khan, *Gendered Disinformation and Its Implications for the Right to Freedom of Expression*, United Nations Human Rights, August 7, 2023,

https://www.ohchr.org/en/documents/thematic-reports/a78288-gen
dered-disinformation-and-its-implications-right-freedom.

18. European Institute for Gender Equality, *Combating Cyber Violence Against Women and Girls*, November 25, 2022, https://eige.europa.eu /publications-resources/publications/combating-cyber-violence-against -women-and-girls.

19. Lara Fontanella et al., "How Do We Study Misogyny in the Digital Age? A Systematic Literature Review Using a Computational Linguistic Approach," *Humanities and Social Sciences Communications* 11, no. 478 (2024), https://www.nature.com/articles/s41599-024-02978-7.

20. Amnesty International, "Crowdsourced Twitter Study Reveals Shocking Scale of Online Abuse Against Women," press release, December 18, 2018, https://www.amnesty.org/en/latest/press-release/2018/12/crowdsourced -twitter-study-reveals-shocking-scale-of-online-abuse-against-women/.

21. Kat Tenbarge, "Elon Musk Made a Kamala Harris Deepfake Ad Go Viral, Sparking a Debate About Parody and Free Speech," *NBC News*, August 1, 2024, https://www.nbcnews.com/tech/misinformation/kamala -harris-deepfake-shared-musk-sparks-free-speech-debate-rcna164119.

22. Euronews, "Deepfake Claiming Kamala Harris Was a Sex Worker Circulating Less Than a Day After Her First Rally," July 24, 2024, https:// www.euronews.com/next/2024/07/24/deepfake-claiming-kamala-harris -was-a-sex-worker-circulating-less-than-a-day-after-her-fir.

23. Security Hero, *2023 State of Deepfakes: Realities, Threats, and Impact*, 2023, https://www.securityhero.io/state-of-deepfakes/.

24. Santiago Lakatos, *A Revealing Picture*, Graphika, December 8, 2023, https://www.graphika.com/reports/a-revealing-picture#download-form.

25. Jim Waterson, "British Female Politicians Targeted by Fake Pornography," *Guardian*, July 1, 2024, https://www.theguardian.com/technology/article /2024/jul/01/british-female-politicians-targeted-by-fake-pornography.

26. Judith Görs, "Baerbock kämpft gegen Fake-News-Welle," n-tv, May 12, 2021, https://www.n-tv.de/politik/Baerbock-kaempft-gegen-Fake-News -Welle-article22551115.html.

27. Mimikama, "Search Results for: 'Baerbock,'" https://www.mimikama .org/?s=baerbock.

28. E. Rosalie Li, Benjamin Shultz, and Nina Jankowicz, *Deepfake Pornography Goes to Washington: Measuring the Prevalence of AI-Generated Non-Consensual Intimate Imagery Targeting Congress*, American Sunlight Project, December 11, 2024, https://static1.squarespace.com/static/6612cb

dfd9a9ce56ef931004/t/67586997eaec5c6ae3bb5e24/1733847451191/ASP
+DFP+Report.pdf.

29. Coralie Kraft, "Trolls Used Her Face to Make Fake Porn: There Was
Nothing She Could Do," *New York Times Magazine*, July 31, 2024,
https://www.nytimes.com/2024/07/31/magazine/sabrina-javellana
-florida-politics-ai-porn.html.

30. Joy Buolamwini and Timnit Gebru, "Gender Shades: Intersectional
Accuracy Disparities in Commercial Gender Classification," *Proceedings
of Machine Learning Research* 81 (2018): 1–15, https://proceedings.mlr
.press/v81/buolamwini18a/buolamwini18a.pdf.

31. Kyle Wiggers and Amanda Silberling, "Meet Unstable Diffusion, the
Group Trying to Monetize AI Porn Generators," TechCrunch, November 17, 2022, https://techcrunch.com/2022/11/17/meet-unstable-diffusion
-the-group-trying-to-monetize-ai-porn-generators/.

32. Ali Winston, "There Are Dark Corners of the Internet: Then There's
764," *Wired*, March 13, 2024, https://www.wired.com/story/764-com
-child-predator-network/.

33. Karen Hao, "The Facebook Whistleblower Says Its Algorithms Are
Dangerous: Here's Why.," *MIT Technology Review*, October 5, 2021,
https://www.technologyreview.com/2021/10/05/1036519/facebook-whis
tleblower-frances-haugen-algorithms/.

34. Cristiano Lima-Strong, Drew Harwell, and Julian Mark, "TikTok
Knew Depth of App's Risks to Children, Court Document Alleges,"
Washington Post, updated October 11, 2024, https://www.washington
post.com/technology/2024/10/11/tiktok-lawsuit-children-addiction
-mental-health/.

35. Robert Wright, "Sam Altman's Imperial Reach," *Washington Post*, October 7, 2024, https://www.washingtonpost.com/opinions/2024/10/07/sam
-altman-ai-power-danger/.

36. Naomi Nix, "Job Rate for Women in Tech Has Hardly Budged Since
2005, EEOC Finds," *Washington Post*, September 11, 2024, https://www
.washingtonpost.com/technology/2024/09/11/big-tech-women-mino
rities-jobs-dei-eeoc/.

37. Victoria Masterson, "Women Founders and Venture Capital—Some
2023 Snapshots," World Economic Forum, March 28, 2024, https://
www.weforum.org/stories/2024/03/women-startups-vc-funding/; Katie
Abouzahr et al., "Why Women-Owned Startups Are a Better Bet,"

Boston Consulting Group, June 6, 2018, https://www.bcg.com/publica
tions/2018/why-women-owned-startups-are-better-bet.

38. Nina Burleigh, "What Silicon Valley Thinks of Women," *Newsweek*,
January 28, 2015, https://www.newsweek.com/2015/02/06/what-silicon
-valley-thinks-women-302821.html.

39. Theodore Schleifer et. al., "Musk Is Going All In to Elect Trump," *New
York Times*, November 8, 2024, https://www.nytimes.com/2024/10/11/us
/politics/elon-musk-donald-trump-pennsylvania.html.

40. Max Chafkin, *The Contrarian: Peter Thiel and Silicon Valley's Pursuit of
Power* (New York: Penguin, 2021).

41. Peter Thiel, "The Education of a Libertarian," *Cato Unbound* (blog),
April 13, 2009, https://www.cato-unbound.org/2009/04/13/peter-thiel
/education-libertarian/.

42. Naomi Nix and Julian Mark, "Mark Zuckerberg Says Corporate Culture
Was 'Neutered' As Meta Scraps DEI," *Washington Post*, January 10, 2025,
https://www.washingtonpost.com/technology/2025/01/10/meta-dei
-affirmative-action-zuckerberg/.

43. Cecilia Kang, "How the Kids Online Safety Act Was Dragged into a
Political War," *New York Times*, July 30, 2024, https://www.nytimes.
com/2024/07/30/technology/kosa-child-online-safety.html#:~:text=The
%20legislation%20would%20require%20social,the%20glorification%20
of%20self%2Dharm.

44. Cyber Civil Rights Initiative, "The 2023 Shield (S.412) Act: An
Explainer," 2023, https://cybercivilrights.org/wp-content/uploads/2023
/06/May-2023-CCRI-SHIELD-Explainer.pdf.

4. THE ROLE MODEL EFFECT OF WOMEN LEADERS

1. Georgia Duerst-Lahti, "Reconceiving Theories of Power: Consequences
of Masculinism in the Executive Branch," in *The Other Elites: Women,
Politics, and Power in the Executive Branch*, ed. M. Borrelli, and J. M.
Martin (Boulder: Lynne Rienner, 1997), 11–32.

2. Pedro Conceição et al., *2023 Gender Social Norms Index* (New York:
United Nations Development Programme, 2023), https://hdr.undp.org
/system/files/documents/hdp-document/gsni202303.pdf, 10–11.

3. Julia Menasce Horowitz and Isabel Goddard, "Women and Political
Leadership Ahead of the 2024 Election," Pew Research Center,

September 27, 2023, https://www.pewresearch.org/social-trends/2023/09/27/views-of-having-a-woman-president/.

4. Daphne van der Pas, Lois Aaldering, and Angela L. Bos, "Looks Like a Leader: Measuring Evolution in Gendered Politician Stereotypes," *Political Behavior* 46 (2024): 1653–1675, https://doi.org/10.1007/s11109-023-09888-5.

5. Christina Ladam, Jeffrey J. Harden, and Jason H. Windett, "Prominent Role Models: High-Profile Female Politicians and the Emergence of Women as Candidates for Public Office," *American Journal of Political Science* 62, no. 2 (2018): 369–381, http://www.jstor.org/stable/26598735; David E. Campbell and Christina Wolbrecht, "See Jane Run: Women Politicians as Role Models for Adolescents," *Journal of Politics* 68, no. 2 (2006): 233–247, https://doi.org/10.1111/j.1468-2508.2006.00402.x.

6. Conceição et al., *2023 Gender Social Norms Index*, 8.

7. Ipsos and Global Institute for Women's Leadership at King's College London, *International Women's Day 2024 Report*, March 2024, https://www.ipsos.com/en-us/millennials-and-gen-z-less-favour-gender-equality-older-generations.

8. Pamela Paxton and Melanie M. Hughes, "Gender and Politics in the 2016 U.S. Election and Beyond," *Socius: Sociological Research for a Dynamic World* 4 (2018), https://doi.org/10.1177/2378023118763844.

9. Christianne Corbett et al., "Pragmatic Bias Impedes Women's Access to Political Leadership," *Proceedings of the National Academy of Science*s 119, no. 6 (2022), https://doi.org/10.1073/pnas.2112616119.

10. Mo Ibrahim Foundation, "Public Opinions on Governance in Africa: Unpacking the Divergence Between Perception and Non-Perception Data," February 2025, https://mo.ibrahim.foundation/sites/default/files/2025-02/public-opinions-on-governance-in-africa.pdf.

11. Amy C. Alexander and Farida Jalalzai, "Symbolic Empowerment and Female Heads of States and Government: A Global, Multilevel Analysis," *Politics, Groups, and Identities* 8, no. 1 (2018): 24–43, https://doi.org/10.1080/21565503.2018.1441034.

12. Ioana M. Latu et al., "Successful Female Leaders Empower Women's Behavior in Leadership Tasks," *Journal of Experimental Social Psychology* 49, no. 3 (2013): 444–448, https://doi.org/10.1016/j.jesp.2013.01.003.

13. Horowitz and Goddard, "Women and Political Leadership Ahead of the 2024 Election."

14. Pew Research Center, "Report: Women and Leadership," January 14, 2015, https://www.pewresearch.org/social-trends/2015/01/14/chapter-2-what-makes-a-good-leader-and-does-gender-matter/.

15. Silvia Bashevkin, *Women as Foreign Policy Leaders: National Security and Gender Politics in Superpower America* (New York: Oxford Studies in Gender and International Relations, 2018).

16. Horowitz and Goddard, "Women and Political Leadership Ahead of the 2024 Election."

17. Conceição et al., *2023 Gender Social Norms Index*, 12.

18. Jana Krause, Werner Krause, and Piia Brönfors, "Women's Participation in Peace Negotiations and the Durability of Peace," *International Interactions* 44, no. 6 (2018): 985–1016, https://doi.org/10.1080/03050629.2018.1492386.

19. Linda Robinson, "Vice President Kamala Harris's Real-World School of Foreign Policy," Women Around the World Blog, July 25, 2024, https://www.cfr.org/blog/vice-president-kamala-harriss-real-world-school-foreign-policy; Linda Robinson, "A Woman in the White House," *Foreign Affairs*, October 31, 2024, https://www.foreignaffairs.com/united-states/woman-white-house-kamala-harris; Linda Robinson, "Kamala Harris and the Glass Cliff," Women Around the World blog, November 8, 2024, https://www.cfr.org/blog/kamala-harris-and-glass-cliff.

20. Aagoth Storvik, "Women on Boards—Experience from the Norwegian Quota Reform," *CESifo DICE Report* 9, no. 1 (2011): 34–41, https://www.ifo.de/DocDL/dicereport111-rm2.pdf.

21. Jessica Kim and Kathleen Fallon, "Making Women Visible: How Gender Quotas Shape Global Attitudes Towards Women in Politics," *Politics and Gender* 19, no. 4 (2023): 981–1006, https://doi.org/10.1017/S1743923X23000089.

22. Farida Jalazai, *Shattered, Cracked, or Firmly Intact? Women and the Executive Glass Ceiling* (New York: Oxford University Press, 2013), 178.

23. Shan-Jan Sarah Liu and Lee Ann Banaszak. "Do Government Positions Held by Women Matter? A Cross-National Examination of Female Ministers' Impacts on Women's Political Participation," *Politics & Gender* 13, no. 1 (2017): 132–162, https://doi.org/10.1017/S1743923X16000490.

24. Alice H. Eagly, "Once More: The Rise of Female Leaders," American Psychological Association, September 8, 2020; Samantha C. Paustian-Underdahl et al., "Gender and Evaluations of Leadership Behaviors:

A Meta-Analytic Review of 50 Years of Research," *Leadership Quarterly* 35, no. 6 (2024), https://doi.org/10.1016/j.leaqua.2024.101822.

25. Linda Robinson, "A Conversation with Prime Minister Mette Frederiksen of Denmark," Council on Foreign Relations, July 9, 2024, https://www.cfr.org/event/conversation-prime-minister-mette-frederiksen-denmark.

26. Alexander Stille, "The Shapeshifter: Who Is the Real Giorgia Meloni?," *Guardian*, September 19, 2024, https://www.theguardian.com/world/2024/sep/19/shapeshifter-who-is-the-real-giorgia-meloni-italy-prime-minister.

27. Brian Kelly, "Italy's PM Meloni Cites Far-Reaching Russian Threat to EU Security," *European Interest*, December 24, 2024, https://www.europeaninterest.eu/italys-pm-meloni-cites-far-reaching-russian-threat-to-eu-security/.

28. Nick Squires, "Giorgia Meloni Tells Court Alleged Deepfake Porn Videos of Her Are 'Form of Violence,'" *Telegraph*, October 8, 2024, https://www.telegraph.co.uk/world-news/2024/10/08/italy-giorgia-meloni-court-deepfake-porn-videos/

29. Reuters, "Italy's Meloni 'Disgusted' by Websites Targeting Women Amid Outcry Over Online Abuse," August 29, 2025, https://www.reuters.com/sustainability/society-equity/italys-meloni-disgusted-by-websites-targeting-women-amid-outcry-over-online-2025-08-29/.

30. European Commission, *2024 Rule of Law Report: Country Chapter on the Rule of Law Situation in Italy*, July 2024, https://commission.europa.eu/document/download/60d79a4f-49cd-4061-a18f-d3a4495d6485_en?filename=29_1_58066_coun_chap_italy_en.pdf.

31. Elizabeth A. Yates and Melanie M. Hughes, "Cultural Explanations for Men's Dominance of National Leadership Worldwide," in *Women Presidents and Prime Ministers in Post-Transition Democracies*, ed. Veronica Montecinos (London: Palgrave Macmillan, 2017), 101–122, https://doi.org/10.1057/978-1-137-48240-2_5.

5. TSAI ING-WEN: CONFRONTING CHINA'S AGGRESSION AGAINST TAIWAN

1. Tsai Ing-Wen, interviewed by Linda Robinson, December 3, 2025. Unless otherwise attributed, all quotes are from this interview and follow-up communications.

2. Anna Fifield, Robin Kwong, and Kathrin Hille, "US Concerned About Taiwan Candidate," *Financial Times*, September 15, 2011, https://www.ft.com/content/f926fd14-df93-11e0-845a-00144feabdc0.

3. Election Study Center, National Chengchi University, "Taiwanese / Chinese Identity (1992/06~2024/06)," July 8, 2024, https://esc.nccu.edu.tw/PageDoc/Detail?fid=7800&id=6961.

4. Global Taiwan Institute, "Taiwan's 'Third Force' Political Parties and the Legacy of the Sunflower Movement," April 6, 2022, https://globaltaiwan.org/2022/04/taiwans-third-force-political-parties-and-the-legacy-of-the-sunflower-movement/.

5. Amber Wang, "Sexist Slurs Mar Taiwan Presidential Elections," Agence France-Presse, December 27, 2019, https://www.courthousenews.com/sexist-slurs-mar-taiwan-presidential-elections/.

6. Shan-Jan Sarah Liu, "Taiwan's First Female President Easily Won Reelection: Are Asian Women Taking Note?," *Washington Post*, February 10, 2020, https://www.washingtonpost.com/politics/2020/02/10/taiwans-female-president-easily-won-reelection-are-asian-women-taking-note/; Joe Buccino, "China Interfered Heavily in Taiwan's Election and Failed—But Next Time It Could Succeed," *The Hill*, January 16, 2024, https://thehill.com/opinion/international/4406585-china-interfered-in-taiwans-election-and-failed-but-next-time-it-could-succeed/.

7. Isabella Steger, "Taiwan's President Is Tired of Getting Trolled for Being a Childless, Single Woman," *Quartz*, updated July 20, 2022, https://qz.com/1659167/taiwan-president-tsai-ing-wen-fends-off-sexist-attacks.

8. Steger, "Taiwan's President Is Tired of Getting Trolled."

9. Thomas J. Shattuck and Benjamin Lewis, "Breaking the Barrier: Four Years of PRC Military Activity Around Taiwan," Foreign Policy Research Institute, October 9, 2024, https://www.fpri.org/article/2024/10/breaking-the-barrier-four-years-of-prc-military-activity-around-taiwan/.

10. Fang-Long Shih, "Taiwan's Culture Wars from 'Re-China-ization' to 'Taiwanization' and Beyond: President Tsai Ing-wen's Cultural Policy in Long-Term Perspective," in *Taiwan in the Era of Tsai Ing-wen: Changes and Challenges*, ed. June Teufel Dreyer and Jacques deLisle (New York: Routledge, 2021), 284–311.

6. MAIA SANDU: DEFENDING MOLDOVA
FROM RUSSIA'S HYBRID WARFARE

1. Maia Sandu, interviewed by Linda Robinson, May 23, 2025, in Chisinau. Unless otherwise attributed, subsequent quotations are from this interview.

2. Maia Sandu, Harvard Kennedy School Commencement Address, May 25, 2022.

3. Elena Sirbu, "The 'Art of Fake News'—How Independent Moldovan Media Fight Russian Disinformation," Voice of America, October 24, 2018, https://www.voanews.com/a/disinfo-moldova-russia/6741966.html.

4. "Vladimir Voronin Says He Will Never Shake Hands with Either of the Presidential Candidates," Infotag.md, November 9, 2016, http://www.infotag.md/politics-en/234404/.

5. Charles Recknagel, "In Moldova, Smears, Orthodox Church Target Pro-EU Candidate Ahead of Runoff," Radio Free Europe/Radio Liberty, updated November 11, 2016, https://www.rferl.org/a/moldova-sandu-smears-orthodox-church-pro-eu-candidate-russia/28108474.html.

6. Recknagel, "In Moldova, Smears, Orthodox Church Target Pro-EU Candidate."

7. Maia Sandu, "Maia Sandu despre mama trimisă în SUA, cu sau fără Transnistria în UE şi preoţii Kremlinului" (in Romanian), interview by Nata Albot, YouTube, September 11, 2024, video, 1:24:13, https://www.youtube.com/watch?v=zIRk5jSMBuw.

8. Ana Maria Touma, "Moldovan President Ridiculed After Putin Joke," *Balkan Insight*, June 6, 2017, https://balkaninsight.com/2017/06/06/moldovan-president-ridiculed-after-putin-joke-06-05-2017/.

9. Keno Verseck, "Moldova Reverses Course," *Deutsche Welle*, November 15, 2019, https://www.dw.com/en/moldova-terminates-its-brief-reform-experiment/a-51272425. The Global Magnitsky Accountability Act of 2016 allows the U.S. president to impose sanctions on foreign individuals and entities for gross violations of human rights or significant corruption.

10. President Sandu, "Message of the President Maia Sandu at the European People's Party's Congress," March 6, 2024, https://presedinte.md/eng/discursuri/mesajul-presedintei-maia-sandu-la-congresul-partidului-popular-european

11. U.S. Department of the Treasury, "Treasury Targets Corruption and the Kremlin's Malign Influence Operations in Moldova," press release, October 26, 2022, https://home.treasury.gov/news/press-releases/jy1049.

12. "Oligarch Sentenced for Role in Stealing $1B From Moldovan Banks," Associated Press, April 14, 2023, https://apnews.com/article/moldova -oligarch-ilan-shor-bank-fraud-chisinau-israel-maia-sandu-e7c9639f 354f27c4975030f7b40629be.

13. Council of Europe Office in Chisinau, "Council of Europe's Anti-Corruption Body Publishes Follow Up Report on the Republic of Moldova," press release, November 28, 2024, https://www.coe.int/en/web/chisinau /-/council-of-europe-s-anti-corruption-body-publishes-follow-up -report-on-the-republic-of-moldova.

14. Wilhemine Preussen, "Russia Is Planning Coup in Moldova, Says President Maia Sandu," *Politico*, February 13, 2023, https://www.politico .eu/article/moldova-president-maia-sandu-russia-attack/; Jon Jackson, "White House 'Deeply Concerned' About Putin's Reported Power Grab," *Newsweek*, updated February 15, 2023, https://www.newsweek .com/white-house-concerned-about-vladimir-putin-moldova-coup -reported-power-grab-1780935.

15. RFE/RL Moldovan Service, "Moldova Expels Russian Diplomat Amid Spying Investigation," Radio Free Europe/Radio Liberty, August 1, 2024, https://www.rferl.org/a/moldova-russian-diplomat-expelled-treason -chisinau-raids/33058909.html.

16. David Gilbert, "A US-Sanctioned Oligarch Ran Pro-Kremlin Ads on Facebook—Again," *Wired*, January 18, 2024, https://www.wired.com /story/ilan-shor-facebook-ads-moldova-elections/. Meta said it banned Shor's party from buying ads, but anonymous accounts continued to do so.

17. Alexander Tanas, "US Sanctions Pro-Russia Governor of Moldova's Gagauzia Region," Reuters, June 12, 2024, https://www.reuters.com /world/us-sanctions-pro-russia-governor-moldovas-gagauzia-region -2024-06-12/.

18. Olga Lautman, "Russia's Remorseless Moldova Campaign Nears a Crescendo," Center for European Policy Analysis, October 30, 2024, https://cepa.org/article/russias-remorseless-moldova-campaign-nears -a-crescendo/.

19. #ShePersisted, *Big Tech and the Weaponization of Misogyny in Moldova's Online Ecosystem*, May 2024, https://she-persisted.org/wp-content /uploads/2024/06/ShePersisted-Moldova-Report-ENG.pdf.

20. Directorate-General for Neighbourhood and Enlargement Negotiations, "Joint Statement by the European Commission and High Representative Josep Borrell on the Second Round of Presidential Elections in

Moldova," European Commission, November 4, 2024, https://neigh
bourhood-enlargement.ec.europa.eu/news/joint-statement-european
-commission-and-high-representative-josep-borrell-second-round
-presidential-2024-11-04_en.

21. Lucjan Kubica, *Moldova's Struggle Against Russia's Hybrid Threats: From Countering the Energy Leverage to Becoming More Sovereign Overall*, Hybrid CoE Working Paper 28, European Centre of Excellence for Countering Hybrid Threats, January 2024, https://www.hybridcoe.fi/wp-content/uploads/2024/01/20240129-Hybrid-CoE-Working-Paper-28-Moldovas-struggle-against-Russias-hybrid-threats-WEB.pdf.

22. Dorin Junghietu, Moldova's energy minister, interviewed by Linda Robinson, May 23, 2025.

23. #ShePersisted, *Big Tech and the Weaponization of Misogyny*.

24. Alina Radu, interviewed by Linda Robinson, May 22, 2025.

25. "Pro-European President Maia Sandu: Force for Change in Moldova," *France24*, November 4, 2024, https://www.france24.com/en/live-news/20241104-pro-european-president-maia-sandu-force-for-change-in-moldova.

7. KAJA KALLAS: STIFFENING EUROPE'S DEFENSES AGAINST RUSSIA

1. Kristi Raik and Merili Arjakas, "Grasping the Opportunity for Small State Leadership: Estonia's Response to the Russian Invasion of Ukraine," *British Journal of Politics and International Relations* 27, no. 4 (2024): 1247–1266, https://doi.org/10.1177/13691481241280368.

2. Kaja Kallas, interviewed by Linda Robinson, June 21, 2023. Other unattributed quotes are from this interview or subsequent follow-up communications.

3. Gabrielle Tétrault-Farber and Tom Balmforth, "Russia Demands NATO Roll Back from East Europe and Stay Out of Ukraine," Reuters, December 17, 2021, https://www.reuters.com/world/russia-unveils-security-guarantees-says-western-response-not-encouraging-2021-12-17/.

4. Kallas, interview.

5. Toomas Sildam, "Kaja Kallas: Debate Cannot Be Allowed to Turn Ugly, or People to Get Hurt," interview, Eesti Rahvusringhääling (Estonian Public Broadcasting), June 30, 2021, https://news.err.ee/160

8262893/kaja-kallas-debate-cannot-be-allowed-to-turn-ugly-or -people-to-get-hurt.

6. Kaja Kallas, "Remarks by Prime Minister Kaja Kallas at the Press Conference with President of Ukraine Volodymyr Zelenski in Zhytomyr," April 4, 2023, Government of the Republic of Estonia, transcript, https:// valitsus.ee/en/news/remarks-prime-minister-kaja-kallas-press-conference -president-ukraine-volodymyr-zelenski.

7. Official website of the President of Ukraine, "Agreement on Security Cooperation and Long-Term Support Between Ukraine and Estonia," June 27, 2024, https://www.president.gov.ua/en/news/ugoda-pro-spivro bitnictvo-u-sferi-bezpeki-ta dovgostrokovu-p-91793.

8. Kaja Kallas, "The Speech of the Prime Minister Kaja Kallas at Victory Day in Viljandi," June 23, 2023, Government of the Republic of Estonia, transcript, https://www.valitsus.ee/en/news/speech-prime-minister-kaja -kallas-victory-day-viljandi-june-23-2023.

9. Government of the Republic of Estonia, "Kallas at the Munich Security Conference: The Crime of Aggression Is a Leadership Crime, the Day of Judgment for Putin and All Other Criminals Will Come," press release, February 17, 2023, https://valitsus.ee/en/news/kallas-munich -security-conference-crime-aggression-leadership-crime-day-judgment -putin-and-all.

10. Kaja Kallas, "Speech by Prime Minister Kaja Kallas on the Government's EU Policy Priorities," December 12, 2023, Government of the Republic of Estonia, transcript, https://www.valitsus.ee/en/news/speech -prime-minister-kaja-kallas-governments-eu-policy-priorities-december -12-2023.

11. Kaja Kallas, "No Peace on Vladimir Putin's Terms," *Foreign Affairs*, December 8, 2022, https://www.foreignaffairs.com/russia/no-peace -putin-terms-kaja-kallas; Ryan Heath and David M. Herszenhorn, "Estonian PM Calls for Strong Sanctions and 'Strategic Patience' in Dealing with Moscow," *Politico*, February 1, 2022, https://www.politico .com/news/2022/02/01/estonia-prime-minister-sanctions-moscow -00004082.

12. Kallas, interview.

13. Stuart Lau and Eva Hartog, "Europe's Next Top Diplomat Is Ready to Be Undiplomatic," *Politico*, December 9, 2024, https://www.politico.eu /article/kaja-kallas-estonia-europe-next-top-diplomat-prime-minister

-brussels-eu-leader/; Ausra Park, "Women in Baltic Politics and Political Leadership," Foreign Policy Research Institute, December 19, 2024, https://www.fpri.org/article/2024/12/women-in-baltic-politics-and-political-leadership/.

8. VJOSA OSMANI-SADRIU: BUILDING DEMOCRACY IN SERBIA'S SHADOW

1. Vjosa Osmani-Sadriu, interviewed by Linda Robinson, April 18, 2024. Unless otherwise attributed, quotes are from this interview and follow-up communications.
2. Vjosa Cerkini, "Vjosa Osmani: A Risk-Taker with Principles," *Deutsche Welle*, September 16, 2021, https://www.dw.com/en/kosovos-president-vjosa-osmani-principled-yet-willing-to-take-risks/a-59197520.
3. United Nations Entity for Gender Equality and the Empowerment of Women (UN Women), *Kosovo Gender Country Profile*, November 2024, https://www.eeas.europa.eu/sites/default/files/documents/2024/UN WOMEN_GEF_ENG.pdf.
4. Osmani, interview.
5. Florent Bajrami and Llazar Semini, "Europe's Youngest Country Kosovo Now 15, But Problems Endure," Associated Press, February 17, 2023, https://apnews.com/article/russia-ukraine-politics-kosovo-government-belgium-european-union-a8b16799f295fadffc33048a93d0ae05.
6. European External Action Service Press Team, "Belgrade-Pristina Dialogue: Agreement on the Path to Normalisation Between Kosovo and Serbia," European Union External Action, February 27, 2023, https://www.eeas.europa.eu/eeas/belgrade-pristina-dialogue-agreement-path-normalisation-between-kosovo-and-serbia_en.
7. Perparim Isufi, "US-Educated Lawyer Becomes Kosovo's Second Female President," *Balkan Insight*, April 5, 2021, https://balkaninsight.com/2021/04/05/us-educated-lawyer-becomes-kosovos-second-female-president/.
8. Council of Europe, "PACE Committee Recommends That Kosovo Be Invited to Become a Member of the Council of Europe," press release, March 27, 2024, https://www.coe.int/en/web/portal/-/pace-committee-recommends-that-kosovo*-be-invited-to-become-a-member-of-the-council-of-europe.

9. Milena Miladinovic, "The New Initiative for Kosovo's Membership in the Council of Europe: An Impossible Mission Without the CSM?," *Kosovo Online*, October 11, 2024, https://www.kosovo-online.com/en/news /analysis/new-initiative-kosovos-membership-council-europe-impossible -mission-without-community.

10. Matija Šerić, "CSM in Kosovo: The Great Serbian Project That Shouldn't Exist—Analysis," *Eurasia Review*, February 27, 2023, https://www.eurasi areview.com/27022023-csm-in-kosovo-the-great-serbian-project-that -shouldnt-exist-analysis/#google_vignette.

11. Nen Si, "Disagreements in the EU About Lifting of Measures Against Kosovo," Euronews Albania, December 15, 2024, https://euronews. al/en/disagreements-in-the-eu-about-lifting-of-measures-against -kosovo/.

9. NATAŠA PIRC MUSAR: REDUCING CONFLICT AT HOME AND ABROAD

1. Danica Fink-Hafner, "Party System Change and Challenges to Democracy in Slovenia," *East European Politics and Societies* 39, no. 1 (2024): 27–51, https://doi.org/10.1177/08883254231219754.

2. Maia de la Baume and Andrew Gray, "EU Conservatives Under Fire Over Soft Line on Slovenian PM," *Politico*, July 1, 2021, https://www .politico.eu/article/eu-conservatives-stand-by-controversial-slovenian -pm-european-peoples-party-janez-jansa/; Mike Smeltzer and Noah Buyon, *Nations in Transit 2022: From Democratic Decline to Authoritarian Aggression* (Washington, DC: Freedom House, 2022), https://freedom house.org/report/nations-transit/2022/from-democratic-decline-to -authoritarian-aggression#Decline; Erik Valenčič, "The Coalition of Hate," *Mladina*, July 23, 2021, https://www.mladina.si/210145/the-coali tion-of-hate/.

3. Nataša Pirc Musar, interviewed by Linda Robinson, June 26, 2023. Unless otherwise attributed, all quotations of her are from this interview.

4. Nika Kovač, interviewed by Linda Robinson, May 23, 2025.

5. Nataša Pirc Musar, "Dr. Nataša Pirc Musar," LinkedIn, accessed December 30, 2024, https://si.linkedin.com/in/dr-nataša-pirc-musar.

6. "Summit of Leaders of the Brdo-Brioni Process: Plenary Session Held in Tivat [Serbia]," *Vijesti*, August 10, 2024, https://www.vijesti.me/vijesti

/politika/727484/samit-lidera-brdo-brioni-procesa-plenarna-sjednica
-odrzana-u-tivtu.

7. Nataša Pirc Musar, "Cooperation Is the Name of the Game," interview
by Matjaž Klemencic, *Region*, November 12, 2023, https://connectingre
gion.com/news/Natasa-pirc-musar-president-of-slovenia-cooperation
-is-the-name-of-the-game/.

8. Pirc Musar, interview.

9. European Western Balkans (EWB), "Montenegrin President at Brdo-
Brijuni Summit in Tivat: The EU Is Not Complete Without the West
ern Balkans," *European Western Balkans*, October 9, 2024, https://europe
anwesternbalkans.com/2024/10/09/montenegrin-president-at-brdo
-brijuni-summit-in-tivat-the-eu-is-not-complete-without-the-western
-balkans/.

10. President of the Republic of Slovenia, "Brdo-Brijuni Leaders' Summit
Underlines the Need for EU Enlargement and Regional Stability," press
release, October 8, 2024, https://www.predsednica-slo.si/en/news/vrh
-voditeljev-procesa-brdo-brioni-poudaril-nujnost-siritve-eu-in-regionalne
-stabilnosti.

11. Leaders of the Brdo-Brijuni Process, "Tivat Presidential Statement,"
October 8, 2024, https://www.predsednica-slo.si/assets/documents
/BrdoBrioni_Tivat-Statement-v2.pdf.

12. Oona A. Hathaway, Maggie M. Mills, and Heather Zimmerman, "How
to Reform the UN Without Amending Its Charter," Carnegie Endowment for International Peace, July 15, 2024, https://carnegieendowment
.org/posts/2024/07/un-reform-security-council-charter-nonamendment
-veto?lang=en.

13. Nataša Pirc Musar, "Statement by the President of the Republic of Slovenia at the 78th Session of the United Nations General Assembly General Debate," September 19, 2023, https://www.predsednica-slo.si/en
/news/statement-by-the-president-of-the-republic-of-slovenia-at-the
-78th-session-of-the-united-nations-general-assembly-general-debate.

14. Global Women Leaders Voices, "Rotation for Equality and Madam
Secretary-General," May 6, 2024, https://www.gwlvoices.org/actions/gw
l-voices-campaign-rotation-for-equality.

15. "President and Prime Minister Engaged in Feud," *Slovenia Times*,
December 18, 2024, https://sloveniatimes.com/41974/president-and-prime
-minister-engaged-in-feud.

10. MIA AMOR MOTTLEY: ADVANCING CLIMATE JUSTICE AND INTERNATIONAL REFORM

1. Abrahm Lustgarten, "The Barbados Rebellion," *New York Times Magazine*, July 27, 2022, https://www.nytimes.com/interactive/2022/07/27/magazine/barbados-climate-debt-mia-mottley.html.

2. Lustgarten, "The Barbados Rebellion."

3. Julian Reingold, "A Brown Tide of Sargassum Is Causing Havoc in Barbados," Dialogue Earth, August 28, 2024, https://dialogue.earth/en/ocean/a-brown-tide-of-sargassum-is-causing-havoc-in-barbados/.

4. BBC News, "Government to pay off WWI debt," https://www.bbc.com/news/business-30306579.

5. Avinash Persaud, "A Q&A with Avinash Persaud, Key Architect of the Bridgetown Agenda and the Loss and Damage Fund," interview by Will Worley, New Humanitarian, January 9, 2024, https://www.thenewhumanitarian.org/interview/2024/01/09/q-and-a-avinash-persaud-key-bridgetown-agenda-loss-and-damage-fund.

6. Rajiv J. Shah, moderator, "Blueprints for a Greener Tomorrow: A Conversation with Prime Minister Mia Mottley of Barbados," Council on Foreign Relations, September 25, 2024, https://www.cfr.org/event/blueprints-greener-tomorrow-conversation-prime-minister-mia-mottley-barbados.

7. Fiona Harvey, "Barbados PM Asks Donald Trump for Face-to-Face Meeting on Climate," *Guardian*, November 13, 2024, https://www.theguardian.com/environment/2024/nov/13/barbados-pm-mia-mottley-donald-trump-climate-meeting-invitation.

8. World Bank, "World Bank Approves Emergency Operation to Support Barbados' Recovery from Hurricane Beryl," press release, November 21, 2024, https://www.worldbank.org/en/news/press-release/2024/11/21/world-bank-approves-emergency-operation-to-support-barbados-recovery-from-hurricane-beryl#:~:text=This%20US%2454%20million%20initiative,face%20of%20future%20climate%20risks.

9. Virginia Furness, "Barbados Completes World First Debt Swap for Climate Resilience," Reuters, December 2, 2024, https://www.reuters.com/business/environment/barbados-frees-up-125-million-via-debt-for-climate-swap-2024-12-02/; Green Climate Fund, "Barbados Launches the World's First Debt-For-Climate-Resilience Conversion," press

release, December 3, 2024, https://www.greenclimate.fund/news/bar
bados-launches-worlds-first-debt-climate-resilience-conversion.
10. World Bank, "Developing Countries Paid Record $1.4 Trillion on For-
eign Debt in 2023," press release, December 3, 2024, https://www.world
bank.org/en/news/press-release/2024/12/03/developing-countries-paid
-record-1-4-trillion-on-foreign-debt-in-2023.

11. WOMEN AND DEMOCRACY

1. Europol, *Facing Reality? Law Enforcement and the Challenge of Deepfakes,
an Observatory Report from the Europol Innovation Lab* (Luxembourg:
Publications Office of the European Union, 2022).
2. Valerie Hudson and Patricia Leidl, *The Hillary Doctrine: Sex & American
Foreign Policy* (New York: Columbia University Press, 2015).

INDEX